FLOWING STREAMS

FLOWING STREAMS

compiled by
Donald Hilton

an Anthology
of Anthologies

NCEC

Other books by Donald Hilton:

Celebrating series
The Millennium Calendar

Compiled or edited by Donald Hilton:

Prayers for the Church Community
(with Roy Chapman)
Liturgy of Life
Living Worship series
Seasons and Celebrations
The Word in the World

Cover design: Peggy Chapman

Published by:
National Christian Education Council
1020 Bristol Road
Selly Oak
Birmingham
B29 6LB

British Library Cataloguing-in-Publication Data:
A catalogue record for this bok is available from the British Library.

ISBN 0-7197-0824-9

First published 1993
Reprinted 1999

Typeset by One and a Half Graphics, Redhill
Printed by Biddles Limited, Guildford

CONTENTS

PREFACE

Countless streams of human experience flow through the Bible narratives. Joy is there, with despair and disillusionment. Anger, fear, and sorrow run alongside gratitude and praise. Conviction ebbs and flows. Many tributaries of faith join to make a broad flowing stream of hope and confidence.

These emotions belong not only to the people whose stories are told in the Bible. They are the same emotions which flow through human life in our own time. Our present life reflects biblical events, and biblical experiences mirror our own.

This anthology broadly follows the story of the Bible. It begins with creation, continues with the questing joy and agony represented by the Exodus and the Exile, celebrates the prophetic hope, and sings songs of joy and sadness. It flows on to hear the Good News with its resulting call to create a new community. It offers glimpses of those truths that speak to our ultimate questions about the meaning of life and death.

Some of the material relates directly to the biblical stories and events; much of it emerges from contemporary experiences which reflect the biblical narrative. The Bible both affirms and challenges our life today. Similarly, contemporary life probes, reflects on, and questions biblical convictions and assumptions.

The National Christian Education Council has published four of my anthologies: *Words to Share, Fresh Voices, A Word in Season,* and *Liturgy of Life.* The first three are now out of print. Regretting the loss of many of the items, the training staff at NCEC suggested creating 'an anthology of anthologies' from that material in the three anthologies which is still useful in promoting Christian Education, and creating Christian worship. **Flowing Streams** is the result. Naturally, I've taken the opportunity to include some new items which constitute over one third of this new anthology.

Donald Hilton

IN THE BEGINNING

In the beginning God created the heavens and the earth. The earth was a vast waste, darkness covered the deep, and the spirit of God hovered over the surface of the water. God said, 'Let there be light, and there was light; and God saw that the light was good.

Genesis 1.1–4a

Where were you when I laid the earth's foundations?
Tell me, if you know and understand.
Who fixed its dimensions? Surely, you know!
Who stretched a measuring line over it?
On what do its supporting pillars rest?
Who set its corner stone in place, while the morning stars sang in chorus and the sons of God all shouted for joy?

Job 38.1–7

You it was who fashioned my inward parts;
you knitted me together in my mother's womb.
I praise you, for you fill me with awe;
wonderful you are, and wonderful your works.
You know me through and through:
my body was no mystery to you,
when I was formed in secret,
woven in the depths of the earth.
Your eyes foresaw my deeds,
and they were all recorded in your book;
my life was fashioned before it had come into being.

Psalm 139.13–16

In the beginning the Word already was. The Word was in God's presence, and what God was, the Word was. He was with God at the beginning, and through him all things came to be; without him no created thing came into being. In him was life, and that life was the light of mankind. The light shines in the darkness, and the darkness has never mastered it.

John 1.1–5

1 To life and immortality

O Lord of every shining constellation
That wheels in splendour through the midnight sky;
Grant us your Spirit's true illumination
To read the secrets of your work on high.

You, Lord, have made the atom's hidden forces,
Your laws its mighty energies fulfil;
Teach us, to whom you give such rich resources,
In all we use, to serve your Holy will.

O life, awakening in cell and tissue,
From flower to bird, from beast to brain of man,
Help us to trace from birth to final issue,
The sure unfolding of your age-long plan.

You, Lord, have stamped Your image on Your creatures,
And though they mar that image, love them still,
Lift up our eyes to Christ, that in His features
We may discern the beauty of your will.

Great Lord of nature, shaping and renewing,
You made us more than nature's sons to be;
You help us tread, with grace our souls enduring,
The road to life and immortality.

Albert F. Bayly

2 God unlimited

What can I say to you, my God? Shall I collect together all the
words that praise your holy Name? Shall I give you all the names
of this world, you, the Unnameable? Shall I call you 'God of my
life, meaning of my existence, hallowing of my acts, my journey's
end, bitterness of my bitter hours, home of my loneliness, you
my most treasured happiness'? Shall I say: Creator, Sustainer,
Pardoner, Near One, Distant One, Incomprehensible One, God
both of flowers and stars, God of the gentle wind and of terrible
battles, Wisdom, Power, Loyalty and Truthfulness, Eternity and
Infinity, you the All-merciful, you the Just One, you Love itself?

Karl Rahner, from *The Name*

3   The legacy of God

God shall have a starring role in my history of the world. How could it be otherwise? If he exists, then He is responsible for the whole marvellous appalling narrative. If He does not, then the very proposition that He might has killed more people and exercised more minds than anything else. He dominates the stage. In His name have been devised the rack, the thumbscrew, the Iron Maiden, the stake; for Him have people been crucified, flayed alive, fried, boiled, flattened; He has generated the Crusades, the pogroms, the Inquisition and more wars than I can number. But for Him there would not be the *St Matthew Passion*, the works of Michaelangelo and Chartres Cathedral.

So how am I to present Him – the invisible all-pervasive catalyst? How am I to suggest to my reader (no informed enlightened reader – a visitor from outer space, let us say) the extraordinary fact that for much of recorded time most people have been prepared to believe in the presidency over all things of an indefinable unassuageable Power?

I shall take a building. A building shaped like a cross, furnished neither for habitation nor defence. I shall multiply this building by a thousand, by ten thousand, by a hundred thousand. It may be as small as a single room; it may soar into the sky. It may be old or it may be new; it may be plain or it may be rich; it may be of stone or it may be of wood or it may be of brick or of mud. This building is in the heart of cities and it is in the wild places of the earth. It is on islands and in deserts and upon mountains. It is in Provence and Suffolk and Tuscany and Alsace and in Vermont and Bolivia and the Lebanon. The walls and furnishings of this building tell stories; they talk of kings and queens and angels and devils; they instruct and they threaten. They are intended to uplift and to terrify. They are an argument made manifest.

The argument is another matter. What I am trying to demonstrate at this point is the amazing legacy of God – or the possibility of God – by way not of ideas but of manipulation of the landscape. Churches have always seemed to me almost irrefutable evidence. They make me wonder if – just possibly – I might be wrong.

Which is how I came once to pray. To kneel down in St George's Pro-Cathedral, Cairo and ask a putative God for forgiveness and help. I was thirty-one.

Penelope Lively, from *Moon Tiger*

4 God in evolution

Five thousand million years ago
Whirling gases cooled and earth was born.
Volcanoes flashed and lightning streaked through
Nights of ebony and silver dawn.
  Wondrous world of past and present;
  Shout a song of joy and praise;
  Living, dying, changing, learning;
  Thanks to God for all his ways.

One thousand million years ago
Oceans ebbed and flowed and life began.
Through coral mazes, jellyfish rainbows,
Tiny animals like jewels swam.

One hundred million years ago
Forests grew and giant ferns unfurled.
On sunbaked land, in humid swamp, lived
Mighty dinosaur, who ruled the world.

Over a million years ago
Skilful hands shaped tools and aimed the spear.
Fast-crackling fire cooked captured prey near
Cave walls carved with nimble-footed deer.

Ann Sutcliffe

5 Small enough?

William Beebee, the naturalist, tells of a ritual through which he
and the late President Roosevelt used to go. After an evening chat
they would step outside and look up at the heavens. Searching
with or without the aid of glasses until they found the faint spot
of light-mist below the lower left-hand corner of the great square
of Pegasus, one of them would recite: 'That is the Spirital Galaxy
of Andromeda. It is as large as our Milky Way. It is one of a
hundred million galaxies. It is seven hundred and fifty thousand
light years away. It consists of one hundred billion suns each larger
than our sun.' After an interval President Roosevelt would grin
and say: 'Now I think we are small enough. Let's go.'

Anon

6   Anonymous God

I grasp at the air
– it slips from my hand;
It's life-giving, there,
invisibly and
        speaks of you, Lord.

The food which I eat
makes energy flow:
my life's made complete
through ways I don't know
        – you're there, Lord God.

I step on the ground:
it holds up my weight!
I walk all around
no plaything of fate
        – you shield me, Lord.

I don't steer the moon
or wind up the sun,
just wake, late or soon
– a new day's begun
        without me, Lord.

Beyond my desires
beyond all my powers
a Spirit inspires
a life-purpose flowers
        – you're there, Lord God.

Ian M. Fraser

7 Ground of our being

Perhaps the root of the trouble is this: the habit of mind which makes us think of God as one item in his universe, as one object among other objects, in the sense in which, for example, a newspaper might declare itself as being for God, king and country, or a theologian might say that although he is interested in many things, God is his chief interest, or a devout person might say that he gives so much time to his work, so much to recreation, and so much to God. Thinking in this way, God is conceived as one being among a multitude of other beings, who stands over against us and is this and not that, here and not there. I have called this a habit of mind. But it is not really an intellectual error, a mistake avoided by the more intelligent among us. Fundamentally it is a failure not in intelligence but in love. It is due to an insufficient apprehension of the charity which is God. And it is the very meaning of our self-inflicted exile from our home, and so from our fulfilment and our peace.

H.A. Williams, from *The True Wilderness*

8 Beauty needs no name

See what a lovely shell,
Small and pure as a pearl,
Lying close to my foot,
Frail, but a work divine,
Made so fairly well
With delicate spire and whorl,
How exquisitely minute –
A miracle of design!

What is it? A learned man
Could give it a clumsy name
Let him name it who can –
The beauty would be the same.

Alfred Tennyson

9   I and my rose

There is a world of wonder in this rose;
God made it, and his whole creation grows
To a point of perfect beauty
In this garden plot. He knows
The poet's thrill
On this June morning, as he sees
His will
To beauty taking form, his word
Made flesh, and dwelling among men.
All mysteries
In this one flower meet
And intertwine,
The universe is concrete
The human and divine,
In one unique and perfect thing, are fused
Into a unity of Love,
This rose as I behold it;
For all things gave it me,
The stars have helped to mould it,
The air, soft moonshine, and the rain,
The meekness of old mother earth,
The many-billowed sea.
The evolution of ten million years,
And all the pain
Of ages, brought it to its birth
And gave it me.
The tears
Of Christ are in it,
And his blood
Has dyed it red,
I could not see it but for him
Because he led
Me to the love of God,
From which all beauty springs.
I and my rose
Are one.

G.A. Studdert Kennedy

10   Harvest plenty

Long, crusty loaves of twisted shapes,
A bowl of eggs, a bunch of grapes;
Michaelmas daisies, mauve and blue,
Gay marigolds and asters too;
A jar of honey, a jug of milk,
Peaches with skins like softest silk;
A box of apples, a bag of plums,
A bunch of bronze chrysanthemums;
Blackberries on a leafy dish,
Marrows as large as you could wish;
A pound of butter, a piece of ham,
A round red cheese, and strawberry jam;
A cabbage with fine, curling leaves,
Wheat, oats and barley in full sheaves;
Baskets of peas still wet with dew,
And runner beans all crisp and new;
Onions, potatoes, carrots, leaks,
Hips and haws with glowing cheeks;
Curved cucumbers, tomatoes red,
And celery with curly head;
Bunches of mint that smell so good,
And gold-fringed bracken from the wood:
For all these things we want to say
Thank you, God, this harvest day.

Marjorie Stannard

11   Seeds

Seeds, bursting from their winter sleep,
Run, their appointed hour to keep.
They strive and thrust, they twist and run,
To lift their hearts towards the sun.
Seeds in their silent winter bed
They lay as cold and still as dead,
Beneath the stiff, white sheets of frost,
Their bodies empty shells and lost.
Beneath the deep, soft quilt of snow
They waited, row on sleeping row;
And when the fingers of the thaw
Tapped gently at each hidden door,
They stirred, the seeds no man can number,
Yet turned again to dark and slumber
Till the first trumpets of the sun,
Tilted to heaven, afresh begun
Their song of spring. The seeds awoke,
Shook off their hard and heavy yoke
Of clay and stone, then, furrow-free,
Leap to fulfil their destiny.

Peter Howard

12   Just suppose

Suppose we're not a fallen people at all,
but people on the way up;
not caterpillars that once were butterflies,
but actually the other way round.

Just suppose we have this wonderful God
who is so much in love with us,
He has drawn us out of the animal kingdom,
giving us the divine spark of His love
to grow into a fire within us and eventually
bring us to oneness with Him.

Just suppose this wonderful God
so totally, crazily in love with us,
first becomes one with His beloved,
taking on a human likeness
to join us in our growing pains,
suffering everything we might suffer,
to show us the truth of the empty chrysalis.

And just suppose that our words of fear
like disobedience and judgement and condemnation,
belong not to a God who is total Love
but to a half-grown people
trying to explain their incompleteness.

Suppose that the only ultimate truth
is that God is the source
and destiny of every soul.
Suppose that everything we are,
all our light and shade, our sin and celebration,
belongs wholly in God's love.
Suppose no one is ever lost to that love.

Wouldn't that be Good News?

Joy Cowley, from *Aotearoa Psalms*

13 The unborn child

Before birth
I felt nothing
I knew nothing.
I was produced
Miraculously
In a small
pocket of flesh
that was part of me.
I lived and yet
was not born.
I was dormant
yet unawakened.
I was safe
Inside my pocket of flesh.
I knew nothing.
I felt nothing
and yet
I was on the threshold
of something
I did not understand
and slowly yet suddenly
I was born into light.
Yet the light
came through shut eyes,
and I was afraid.

Barbara Blake, 15 years

14 Stress of life

O, the effort of being born,
Lungs expanding, the first breath drawn.
O, the strain of trying to walk,
And the frustration of learning to talk.
O, the wonder of childhood eyes,
O, the torture of teenage whys.
Knowing the difference between right and wrong,
And the nightmares of the hydrogen bomb.
Rush, tear, noise and clamour,
Deadens all this so-called glamour.
O, the agony of first love spurned,
O, the joy of love returned.
O, the stress of family life,
Worry, work, toil and strife.
Then when all have left the fold,
What is left?
Despair of growing old.

Christopher Pinch

15 Gift for a child

I wish this child to have a gift –
Perhaps of love?
And if it is granted
Love may turn, its other side is hate
And hate brings men to war
And mothers mourn.

Perhaps for art?
To paint a masterpiece in paint or words,
Inspire young fools to fight
And burn the dead within their doors!

Perhaps of intelligence?
This gift of life could lead a man to search
And find – a way of death
So vast, so terrible,
My earth may be destroyed!

Perhaps the skill to build?
But bombs and missiles with blasphemous names
Are built –
From building rockets to conquer space,
To building bombs to conquer man –
Even this gift may turn to sin!

Perhaps the gift to learn
To live with other men
To learn to love the life we have
To learn kindness
And crush war and suffering with love –

So, love is the answer
The best gift
The gold of life.

Robert Bramley, 15 years

16 In the beginning, God made laughter

He made it for Adam,
    when the winter came
    and the leaves started to wither;
He made it for Eve,
    when her children asked
    where their mum came from;
He made it for Methusaleh,
    when the time came to blow out the candles
    on his birthday cake;
He made it for Mrs. Noah,
    when her husband first mentioned
    his amphibious zoo;
He made it for Abraham,
    when a year off a hundred
    he was asked to walk the world;
He made it for Sarah,
    when she eavesdropped on an angel
    and giggled until she was pregnant;
He made it for Moses
    when the sheep raised their heads
    in confusion at his stutter;
He made it for Miriam,
    when she danced on dry land
    as a sign of liberation;
He made it for wee David,
    when Saul offered to make him
    the youngest lance corporal;
He made it for big Goliath,
    when he first glimpsed the cause
    of impending rigor mortis;
God made laughter for himself
    when his children on earth
    took themselves too seriously;
And he gave it to Jesus
    to share with his friends,
    to use in his stories,
    to praise in young children,
    to bring to the sad.
So, we dare not, in our wisdom,
doubt that God inhabits humour,
nor condemn him to be dour
like some bankrupt undertaker.
From his Spirit issues joy,
and that fruit is for our healing.

Source unknown

17 If you have ears . . .

Bubbling water,
Bubbling stream,
Howling wind,
Hissing stream.

Crackling wood,
Clanking chain,
Pealing bells,
Pattering rain.

Noises, noises,
All around,
Listen! Listen!
Can you hear a sound?

Joan Sabin

18 Rich delight

The wren's sweet song;
The cuckoo's cry;
Larks singing
In the clear blue sky;
My dog's gay bark;
Wind in the wheat
On golden days
Of summer heat;
The babbling murmur
Of a stream
Over the stones,
Coolly a-gleam;
The hum of insects;
Robin's call
When autumn leaves
Begin to fall;
Sparrows' lively
Chirruping
When crumbs to them
Each day I fling;
The zoom of bees
In lazy flight –
These sounds to me
Bring rich delight!

Malcolm Hemphrey

19 Noise

I like noise:
The whispering of branches.
The weeping of willows.
The flap of our bedclothes.
The thud of our pillows.
The thumping of engines.
The screeching of brakes.
The noises of people
Who sit munching cakes.
The crashing of dustbins.
The singing of songs.
The jingle of teabells
And loud dinner gongs.
The turning of pages.
The rattle of pens.
The screeching and squawking
Of roosters and hens.
The howl of the north wind.
The beat of the rain.
The incessant turn
Of the black weather vane.
The thumping of footsteps.
The clicking of heels.
The noises that cards make
When somebody deals.
The lapping of oceans.
The gurgling of streams.
The noise of supporters
Who yell for their teams.
The creaking our house makes
When everything's dark.
And the rusty complaints
From the swings in the park.
The jingle of money
In shopkeepers' tills.
And the rustle from cheque books
As folk pay their bills.
The screams from the girls
And the yells of the boys.
The laughter of children
Who play with their toys.
– I like noise.

Rachael Chaldecott, 14 years

20 Listen hard

Be quiet now.
  Birds are singing,
  Bells are ringing,
  Postmen knocking,
  Listen hard.

Be still now.
  Rain is dripping,
  Wind is blowing,
  Car doors slamming,
  Listen hard.

Be silent now.
  Planes are flying,
  Ships are hooting,
  Dockers working,
  Listen hard.

Be hushed now.
  Cows are mooing,
  Sheep are bleating,
  Tractor chugging,
  Listen hard.

Be gentle now.
  Doves are cooing,
  Babes are crying,
  People sighing,
  Listen hard.

Donald Hilton

21 Common senses

The sound of the sea on weather worn rocks.
Lying in sun drenched bracken.
Climbing the fells in the misty morning.
Swimming in the cool clear ghylls and tarns.

The smell of tar.
Playing games in fresh green fields.
Listening to the sound of the wind
whistling in the gorse and the sound of birds.

As I return home in the evening
the greetings of my dog.
The lavish tickling of his warm
tongue against my face.

Graham Kitchen, 11 years

22 The white stick

Red bricks, grey slate, cream road.
My eyes ached,
Same old walls, same old houses,
Old churches, old ships, old railings,
Everything was old,
No grass or trees.
I was sick, for want of the country;
I looked around me.
My eyes were drawn
To a solitary figure, walking slowly.
I saw in the figure's hand a white stock.
Blindness.
I imagined the eternal blackness.
What had he done.
To earn this mockery of man?
The figure turned into another street,
Tapping, feeling for the next shape,
Dependent on the white stick.
I wanted to help him.
What use was I? Just to show him the next corner.

Anon, 15 years

23 Blind sight

I have walked with people whose eyes are full of light, but who see nothing in wood, sea, or sky, nothing in the city streets, nothing in books. What a witless masquerade is this seeing! It were better far to sail for ever in the night of blindness, with sense and feeling and mind, than to be thus content with the mere act of seeing. They have the sunset, the morning skies, the purple of the distant hills, yet their souls voyage through this enchanted world with a barren stare.

Helen Keller

24 The blind leading

I saw the fog grow thick,
  Which soon made blind my ken;
It made tall men of boys,
  And giants of tall men.

It clutched my throat, I coughed;
  Nothing was in my head
Except two heavy eyes
  Like balls of burning lead.

And when it grew so black
  That I could know no place,
I lost all judgement then,
  Of distance and of space.

The street lamps, and the lights
  Upon their halted cars,
Could either be on earth
  Or be the heavenly stars.

A man passed by me close,
  I asked my way, he said,
'Come, follow me, my friend' –
  I followed where he led.

He rapped the stones in front,
  'Trust me,' he said, 'and come';
I followed like a child –
  A blind man led me home.

W.H. Davies

25 To touch

I often run the sole of my bare foot
    along the cat's back,
  Velvet, warm and soft.
Silk is glorious to touch and rub:
  Soft, shiny paper.
Lush grass is nice to run over.
  Milk tops are sensational to rub.
The rubber underside of a ground-sheet;
  Worn, shiny wood.
Slippery tiles,
  Also smooth stones are beautiful
    to touch, and
Metal and
  Canvas, lovely rough canvas.

Stephen Taylor (9 years)

26 To feel

For the feel of warm wool, soft to the skin,
And the polished touch of smooth wood.
  We praise and thank the Creator of all things.

For the gentle stroke of cats' fur,
And the touch of a hamster's coat,
  We praise and thank the Creator of all things.

For the bite of cold snow, hard-pressed into a ball,
And the trickle of sand through the fingers,
  We praise and thank the Creator of all things.

Donald Hilton

27 To smell

Why is it that the poets tell
So little of the sense of smell?
These are the odours I love well:

The smell of coffee, freshly ground;
Or rich plum pudding, holly crowned;
Or onions fried and deeply browned.

The fragrance of a fumy pipe;
The smell of apples, newly ripe;
And printers' ink on leaden type.

Woods by moonlight in September
Breathe most sweet; and I remember
Many a smoky camp-fire ember.

Camphor, turpentine, and tea,
The balsam of a Christmas tree,
These are the whiffs of gramarye –
A ship smells best of all to me!

Christopher Morley

28 To taste

Fresh baked bread, newly from the oven,
Rich plum pudding, fat and round,
Hot buttered crumpets, smooth dark chocolate,
Warm baked potatoes, oven browned.

Ice cream sodas, cold and creamy,
Sponge treacle puddings, fluffy and light,
Large juicy melons sprinkled with sugar,
Hot yellow pancakes, tossed just right.

Hot roasted chestnuts, straight from the embers,
Freshly made coffee, fragrant and strong,
Thick lentil soup poured from the saucepan,
Crisp sausage rolls, round, thin and long.

Round cream doughnuts, jammy and gooey,
Beef stew with dumplings tasty and thick,
Soft currant bread, spread thickly with butter,
Ripe crunchy apples, just take your pick.

All of these are my favourite eatables,
Sticky, stodgy, like glue or like paste,
Some of them crispy, gooey and fluffy,
Because all of this poem is all about taste.

Vanessa Lincoln, 12 years

29 Ways of learning

'Today I will teach you roses.
Look!' I looked
And saw a bush, in subtle balance,
Pleasure to the eye,
With golden flowers, swaying in the breeze.
Then I looked closer, saw how it was made,
Each single part built up, to the last molecule.
So. This is a rose.

'Now close your eyes
And let me lead you.
Here. Inhale. What do you smell?'
The scent was sweet, intoxicating,
Wayward, elusive in the wind.
This too is a rose?

So sweet the scent, how must it taste?
'Bend down and eat, if you desire.'
I bent, and ate, and found it hard.
It was a bitter swallowing.
My mouth was torn and bleeding.
And this is a rose?

'Since you are pain-struck and perplexed
Turn once again. Now sit,
Be very still and listen.
So I did
As I was bid,
And heard the wind among the leaves.
No more.
The life of cell and bud and root
To me was silence, imperceptible.
I don't know how to listen to a rose.

'There's only one thing left to do,
So touch it,
Hold it gently in your hands,
Let it touch you.'
I can't tell what a rose is
In itself.
But, if it will,
I may submit to let it teach me
As the wind blows
Still.

W.S. Beattie

30 Creation fulfilled

If we are images of a creator, then it is up to us to create, and to create good things too. All the things that happened in those distant millions of years were only the beginning. The stars and the Sun, the Earth and the volcanoes, the water and the early living creatures, all these were the beginning, paving the way for the great time when we ourselves could share in the creation of everything that is good and fine.

We live at the end of the beginning. The world will go on into the future, and what is created upon it in the way of good things and bad things depends no longer upon God alone, but on the way in which each one of us does something to make the creation still more wonderful than it was before, helping to fulfil the purpose of the millions of years which lie behind us.

Roger Pilkington

31 God's glory

Can we not say to the young apprentice who has just learnt the use of a high precision lathe, and is thrilled at his new ability to use so apparently heavy and bulky a machine to prepare a piece of metal to a given shape with an accuracy of one ten-thousandth of an inch, that God is equally thrilled, and that this sheer joy in the situation is not wholly different from that of the angels who behold God's glory and rejoice?

C.A. Coulson

32 Genesis and Bethlehem

He penetrates the amazing vastness of Space
Light-Bringer
Love-Maker
Gracious Purposer and Creative Intelligence
Taking human form
Risking rejection
To make us
Children of God.

Anon

33 Action

We all love doing things,
Doing and making,
Cooking and baking,
Painting and drawing,
Hammering, sawing,
Jumping and running,
Joking and funning,
Swinging,
And singing,
And rushing about,
Letting off steam in a shout:
For these and a hundred things more
That You love to see us enjoy,
Thank You, God!
Hurrah!

Lilian Cox

34 A heritage

In eighteen hundred eighty eight
Michael Robbins made a gate;
Struck it true and struck it straight.

Michael Robbins, hale and free,
As fine a man as you might see;
Smith and sexton both was he.

"Praise God from whom all blessings flow!"
He sang. The gate began to grow.
"Praise Him, all creatures here below!"

Simple, gentle, sturdy, kind
Michael Robbins left behind
Treasure for the honest mind;
For while the wind goes shouting by,
And men are born, grow old and die,
His gate stands talking to the sky.

M.J. Martyn

35 Effort

I had a moment of mixed joy and anguish, when my mind took over. It raced well ahead of my body and drew my body compellingly forward. I felt that the moment of a lifetime had come. There was no pain, only a great unity of movement and aim. The world seemed to stand still, or did not exist.

I felt at that moment that it was my chance to do one thing supremely well. I drove on, impelled by a combination of fear and pride.

Those last few seconds seemed never-ending. The faint line of the finishing tape stood ahead as a haven of peace, after the struggle. The arms of the world were waiting to receive me if only I reached the tape without slackening my speed. I leapt at the tape like a man taking his last spring to save himself from the chasm that threatens to engulf him.

My effort was over and I collapsed almost unconscious with an arm on either side of me.

Roger Bannister
The first man to run a mile in four minutes

36 True greatness

A person can never get true greatness by paying for it. It is nice to have good clothes, it makes it a lot easier to act decent, but it is a sign of true greatness to act decent when you have not got them, just as good as if you had.

One time, when mother was a little girl, they had a bird at their house called Bill that broke its leg. They thought they would have to kill him, but next morning they found him, sort of sideways, on his good leg – singing. That was true greatness.

Once there was a woman that had done a big washing and hung it on the line. The line broke and let it all down in the mud, but she did not say a word, only did it all over again. This time she spread it on the grass where it could not fall; but that night a dog with dirty feet ran over it. All she said was, "Aint it queer that he did not miss nothing". That was true greatness. But it is only people who have done washing that know it.

Anon. Written by a schoolgirl, 13 years, in 1913

37 The grace of touch

The Sistine touch gave life, the vital spark
Across the void to Adam. But in light or dark
We feel the touch, not coolly held in point,
Which, known, confirms our being, sinner, fool and saint.
      Touch of your hand.

Warm comfort when a mother holds a child,
Thrashing at night caught in a net of dreaming wild,
A touch the madman knew among the tombs
When Legion fled, leaving a mind of ordered rooms.
      Touch of your hand.

The surgeon's touch, guiding the glinting steel,
Reaches the heart of pain to cauterise and heal
The inner sore. A therapeutic cut
The temple feels, excising cancer from the gut,
      Touch of your hand.

Untouchable the leper sees the crowd
Withdraw, until a Francis in delight declares he's proud
To run his hand across the noduled face,
And clasp our brother leper in a hug of grace.
      Touch of your hand.

Knowledge and love our fingers sensitise,
But rarely do we wait to feel with lovers' eyes.
And when like Thomas doubting you I stand
You will reach out, across this crowded no-man's-land,
      To touch my hand.

Bernard Thorogood

QUESTS AND QUESTIONS

By faith Abraham obeyed the call to leave his home for a land which he was to receive as a possession; he went away without knowing where he was go to.

Hebrews 11.8

He found his people in a desert land,
in a barren, howling waste.
He protected and trained them,
he guarded them as the apple of his eye.
As an eagle watches over its nest,
hovers over its young,
spreads its pinions and takes them up,
and bears them on its wings,
the Lord alone led his people,
no alien god at his side

Deuteronomy 32.10-12

It was at this time that Jesus came from Nazareth in Galilee and was baptised in the Jordan by John. As he was coming up out of the water, he saw the heavens break open and the Spirit descend on him, like a dove. And a voice from heaven: 'You are my beloved Son; in you I take delight.'

At once the Spirit drove him out into the wilderness, and he remained there forty days tempted by Satan. He was among the wild beasts; and angels attended to his needs.

Mark 1.9-13

Calling the Twelve together he gave them power and authority to overcome all demons and to cure diseases, and sent them out to proclaim the kingdom of God and to heal the sick. 'Take nothing for the journey,' he told them, 'neither stick nor pack, neither bread nor money; nor are you to have a second coat. When you enter a house, stay there until you leave that place. As for those who will not receive you, when you leave their town shake the dust off your feet as a warning to them.' So they set out and travelled from village to village, and everywhere they announced the good news and healed the sick.

Luke 9.1-6

38 Morning hymn

Kia ora, my Friend God.
I give to you the voyage of this day,
that to be which is already yours,
adding to it my rejoicing,
a shout of praise. Amen. Amen.
You are the wind: fill up my sails.
You are the water: run fast beneath my keel.
And I will sing in the wind
and dance over the water,
God my friend, oh God my Friend.
You are the light: enfold me.
You are the darkness: embrace me.
You are the pain: hollow me.
You are love: overflow me.
The storms of change are you,
and the peace of tranquil waters.
You are all these things, Friend God,
and I thank you. Amen. Amen.
May I journey without fear
through all your seasons.
In emptiness let me find fullness,
In imprisonment let me find freedom.
Render me passive in your will
and I shall be most active,
moving with you in everything,
seeing you in everything,
knowing you in everything.
Amen. Amen.

Joy Cowley, from *Aotearoa Psalms*

39 Yonder wicket-gate

Now I saw, upon a time, when he was walking in the fields, that he was (as he was wont) reading in his book, and greatly distressed in his mind; and as he read, he burst out as he had done before, crying, What shall I do to be saved?

I saw also that he looked this way, and that way, as if he would run; yet he stood still, because (as I perceived) he could not tell which way to go. I looked then, and saw a man named Evangelist coming to him, and asked, Wherefore dost thou cry?

He answered, Sir, I perceive, by the book in my hand, that I am condemned to die, and after that to come to judgement; and I find that I am not willing to do the first, nor able to do the second.

Then said Evangelist, If this be thy condition, why standest thou still? He answered, Because I know not whither to go. Then he gave him a parchment roll, and there was written within, Fly from the wrath to come.

The man therefore read it, and, looking upon Evangelist very carefully, said, Whither must I fly? Then said Evangelist pointing with his finger over a very wide field, Do you see yonder Wicket-gate? The man said, No. Then said the other, Do you see yonder shining light? He said, I think I do. Then said Evangelist, Keep that light in your eye, and go up directly thereto, so shalt thou see the gate; at which, when thou knockest, it shall be told thee what thou shalt do.

John Bunyan, from *Pilgrim's Progress*

40 Roads

I enjoy looking at other people's roads.
They are different from mine
and yet basically the same.
They all facilitate journey
from here to there, self to other,
and they are all inter-connected.

The fact that I love my own road
with its comfortable landmarks
and familiar faces,
doesn't restrict my appreciation
of someone else's neighbourhood.

And if I go into another area
and walk a mile or two with someone else,
I return as a larger being.
The love of my own road is deepened,
the appreciation of other roads is widened
and I am blessed in the knowledge
that all roads lead to God.

Joy Cowley, from *Aotearoa Psalms*

41 'I am the way'

Thou art the Way.
Hadst thou been nothing but the goal,
   I cannot say
If thou hadst ever met my soul.

   I cannot see –
I, child of process – if there lies
   An end for me,
Full of repose, full of replies.

   I'll not reproach
The road that winds, my feet that err.
   Access, approach
Art thou, Time, Way, and Wayfarer.

Alice Meynell

42 What are the facts?

When you are studying any matter or considering any
philosophy, ask yourself only what are the facts and what is
the truth that the facts bear out. Never let yourself be
diverted either by what you would wish to believe or by what
you think would have beneficial social effects if it were
believed. But look only at what are the facts.

Bertrand Russell

43 The rhythm of God

Eternal God,
Let darting insight pierce the commonplace of every day,
imagination find new soaring wings,
perception probe the surface of well-trodden life,
so that out of fading patterns,
weathered by customs loved too long,
we find the newer rhythm of your purpose,
and finding it,
begin to share the life you freely offer.

Donald Hilton

44 To Colonel Alexei Leonov
(The first man to walk in space)

So you stepped out of your space capsule
Into nothing
Where man had never been before
You hovered in a partial vacuum
Hazarding all upon a theory.
No one had done before what you have done
No one could be quite sure what you would meet.
Of course they made their calculations,
Caution had carefully prepared for what might be,
But no one could be sure.
Until you clambered out
Man's dream remained
A wistful longing, unfulfilled.
But you made out of it
Reality.

And so you gave man freedom to explore
A medium beyond
The envelope of atmosphere, his home.
New worlds are his
Not only hemispheres,
Infinite of space
with only time to check his wanderings.
And all this came
From opening a door
And stepping into
The Unknown.

Lord, make us men of faith:
Faith to trust in what we hope for,
Faith to live by what we cannot prove
Until we risk ourselves upon it
With our lives.

Teach us by man's conquest of the world,
By those who ventured on a dream
And found new continents, new truth, new power
By faith.

Teach us to trust the hopes we have been given
The hope of peace and welfare for mankind,
The hope that love means more than hate,
The hope that death is not the cynical denial
Of all that man has hoped for.

Teach us to take these and to live by them
And so to find that liberty from fear,
And live as free men in a world
Where man is called to live by faith
Or to withdraw
A frightened beast, defeated by reality.

Teach us to live
As Jesus lived
Who took the hopes of men
And made them real
By stepping out of safe convention
Into love.
And so he gave us freedom
By his faith.

Jim Bates

45 Follow truth and follow Christ

Safety is not behind but before, and the demand which
should ring ever more loudly in our ears is to ensure more
earnestly, more humbly, more patiently, more utterly in the
spirit of love and with a more exclusive regard to the interests
of truth. So shall we follow him who is True and see the
glory of his Kingdom which is Love.

John Oman

46   The quiet pool

There is within each of us
a quiet clear pool of living water
fed by the one deep Source
and inseperable from it,
but so often hidden
by a tangle of activity
that we may not know
of its existence.

We can spend the proverbial forty years
wandering in strange deserts,
sinking unrewarding wells
and moving on, driven by our thirst,
but when we stop still long enough
to look inside ourselves, really look
beyond our ideas about water
and what and where it should be,
we discover it was with us all the time,
that quiet clear pool which is ageless,
the meaning of our existence
and the answer to all wanderings.

And as we drink,
we know what Jesus meant when he said
we'd never be thirsty again.

Joy Cowley, from *Aotearoa Psalms*

47 Evil unleashed

Another memory:

Raphael's brother Hayim was describing the massacre at Kolomey. The men listened in disbelief. And he watched them as they listened. Like the others, he wondered if his poor brother had lost his mind. Hayim told how the Germans ordered young Jews to dig a vast pit in the forest. And how meticulously they organized the massacre. As the men listened, they could hear the sobs of the mothers, they could see the fear of the children. Hayim told how some prayed and others remained silent. Raphael listened but he was too young to understand. He understood the words, but not the enormity of their meaning. It was as though the words detached themselves from one another and flew off in different directions. A clear blue day, the crackling of machine guns, men shooting, men dying, women watching as their children were murdered. It all seemed unreal.

After the men left, Raphael asked, "How can this be true? How can man be so cruel?"

"Remember," replied the father, "once evil is unleashed, anything is possible."

That night, curled up on his cot, Raphael could not sleep. The image of evil unleashed on mankind tormented him. Whose fault was it? Whose responsibility? Horror on this scale implicated not only man but God as well. Only God could vanquish evil, halt the massacres, end the wars. Why didn't He? Could He be on the side of the killers? Raphael rejected that notion. God on the side of evil? Unthinkable. Was He not the opposite of evil? He told himself that he would never accept the idea that God could be cruel. Man could be cruel, not God. He was convinced of it. But then, what about the killings in Kolomey? Yes, that was worse than the concept of a cruel or indifferent God.

Elie Wiesel, from *Twilight*

48 As if you were not there

As if you were not there,
The skies ignite and thunder,
Rivers tear their banks asunder,
Thieves and nature storm and plunder:
All beware,
As if you were not there.

As if you were not there,
Famine and flood together
Usher death, disease and terror;
Stricken mothers wonder whether
God heeds prayer,
As if you were not there.

As if you were not there,
We televise the dying,
Watch the helpless victims crying,
Salve our consciences by sighing
'Life's unfair!'
As if you were not there.

As if you were not there,
Your Son, when faith defied him,
Faced a crowd which crucified him,
Leaving friends who had denied him
In despair,
As if you were not there.

Because he rose again
And showed God's love is faster
Than the ultimate disaster,
We entreat you now to master
Strife and pain,
Because he rose again.

Iona Community

49 Woof, Woof

I can't quite make you human beings out.
All I can do is love and trust
And marvel at the things you seem to want.
I'm just your dog,
My treasure is this bone.
I worry at it endlessly,
Lose it, and search, and dig it up again.
This is the thing on which my heart is set.
I wonder what, in all your wealth,
You have as precious.

Friend,
We are not that much different.
There is a savour that I too have smelt,
And struggled for a grip on it.
How can I make you understand?
I'll put it simply:
It's as if
This whole world,
Everything I see, all I experience,
Were the bone
For me to worry at,
And God the marrow at its core.

I'm just a man.
All I can do is love and trust
And marvel at the things He seems to want.
I wonder, shall I ever understand
What is His treasure?

W.S. Beattie

50 Walking on water

Walking on water looks difficult,
but I have seen it done.

Those with enough grief to sink them
have kept on –
drawn by an invisible source
of strength
they were not let down.

Crossing this sea
some swim
and others drown,
but some there are
walking on water.

Cecily Taylor

51 Pioneers

God, we give thanks for the pioneers of the human race, who believed that we could travel on the waters, and did not rest until they had made boats; who believed that we could travel in a horseless chariot, and laboured through difficulty and scorn until an engine was built; who believed that we could fly, and persevered until at last the air was conquered; who believed that space was open to our exploration, and built rockets and capsules with great daring.

We thank you for those in the world today who believe that cancer can be banished, and poverty and war abolished, and leisure and education and comfort provided freely for all.

Bless these bold spirits; strengthen their hearts and their arms. Save us from ever scoffing, and may we share their faith and lend our aid towards the accomplishments of the new triumphs which you have put into the dreams and hopes of humankind.

S.G. Hedges (adapted)

52 Eureka!

Some algebraic formulae caught my eye . . . it was part of a paper by a Mr. N. Bohn, of whom I had never heard . . . I sat down and began to read. In half an hour I was in a state of excitement and ecstasy, such as I have never experienced before or since in my scientific career. I had just finished a year's work revising a book on Modern Electrical Theory. These few pages made everything I had written entirely obsolete. That was a little annoying, no doubt. But the annoyance was nothing to the thrill of a new revelation, such as must have inspired Keats' most famous sonnet. And I had so nearly missed the joy of discovering this work for myself, and rushing up to the laboratory to tell everyone else about it . . . twenty years have not dampened my enthusiasm.

N.R. Campbell

53 Open to learn

'Brainwashing' and 'indoctrination' are to be repudiated, but this does not mean that the reasoned teaching of Christian doctrine is to be left out; indeed, how could any pupils be satisfied with an understanding of any religion that did not include a careful explanation of its beliefs? But the pupil is not a blank page upon which the teacher writes indelibly: he is a person who, however much he is assisted, must discover for himself whatever truth he eventually holds. The aim is not the production of adolescents who can give slick and correct answers to a series of catechetical questions but the development of adults who will continue to reflect seriously upon the fundamental problems of human existence and to arrive at the decisions which life calls for, both theoretical and practical, in a spirit of responsibility. Teaching must therefore be open-ended, not in the superficial sense that teachers and pupils should pretend that they start in any discussion from no point of view, no belief, no conviction, nor that the authority of the teachers, derived from their greater knowledge and experience is ignored, but in the sense that enquiry is genuine, search for greater understanding is always present, and a real coming together of minds, a pooling of thoughts and of evidence, is always desired.

Learning for Life

54 To choose is to grow

For the first years of your life you rely on grown-ups, who know all that happens or does not happen in the world, what you must do and when and how you must do it. Then youth comes. Everything in the world turns out to be inconstant and changing, and not always reasonable. You begin to notice that grown-ups are not as reliable as all that; they often make mistakes, and hesitate, and disagree with one another, sometimes even contradict themselves, and do not know nearly all there is to know. Now you often have to do things on your own initiative and at your own risk. Roads divide, and at each cross-roads you are faced with the difficult problem of choosing your own path. You have already gathered a certain experience of life, and are impatient and hungry for more.

Samuel Marshak

55 Faith's paintbox

Jesus is the normal child in the sense that his childhood is normative. There is a pattern of human childhood in the childhood of Jesus. The essence of this pattern is not that 'Christian children all must be, mild, obedient, good as he'. The child Jesus does not tell today's children how to behave. But the childhood of Jesus does confer on human childhood infinite worth. If the humanity of Jesus was as perfectly expressed by his childhood as by his manhood, then it must be affirmed that there is potentially for every child, at every age, an appropriate Christian maturity. Whether at ten years, ten months, or ten days there is the right relationship to God fitted to that age.

When Christians seek to nurture their young into Christian faith, they literally do not fully know what they are nurturing them into. They only know the resources but not the use which will be made of them. What we pass on to our children is not the painting but the paintbox.

The Child in the Church

56 Changing faith

Christian nurture is therefore very different from the inculcation of a fixed set of beliefs and a fixed set of rules of conduct (which is an idea one might easily get from looking at some older catechisms).

The Christian way is not something fixed and unchanging. A living way is not a way that never changes, but one which remains true to itself. The mark of a living tradition is not immutability but continuity. Christian growth is thus not a matter of simply taking over the tradition, or of swallowing what it offers us, but rather of *responding* to what is offered. As we grasp it, make it our own, it does something to us. But at the same time *we* do something to *it*, as we interpret it to meet our own needs, and as we put to it the questions which face us now. We become new people by walking in the Christian way, but the way itself is continually renewed by those who walk in it.

The Child in the Church

57 I wonder

I wonder, I wonder, I wonder why,
Why sun and moon are up so high.
Oh I wonder, I wonder,
How does it thunder?
It makes me frightened when it lightens.
I wonder how moths
Make silk cloths.
I wonder how it changes from day to night
And how it changes to morning light.
I wonder how fishes swim in the sea
And how we get honey from the bee.
I wonder how we shout and talk
And how we run and how we walk.
I wonder, I wonder, I wonder why,
Why sun and moon are up so high.

Julie Rains, 10 years

58 Questions

Where do words go when we speak?
Why do seven days make a week?
Where does the light of the sun go at night?
Why is the moon's light never so bright?
How can the flowers break through the ground?
How do they know there is no snow around?
How do the dark clouds change into rain?
What makes the clouds dark and then white again?
How many questions can there be?
As many as there are fish in the sea.

Karen Jones, 9 years

59   Me

What am I?
 A boy.

Why am I?
I can never arrive
At a satisfactory
 Answer
As to why
 I am.
But there must be a reason,
For without a reason,
What is the point of
 Me.
Being around to eat
 Good food
And using up
Useful space?

So,
Why
Am I?

Anon

60   If I was a caterpillar

If I was a caterpillar
What would I do?
Would I live on my own
Would I know what to do
Would I know if I saw you
When I was first born
Would I know where to go
if I sat on a lawn
Would I know if I changed
Would I know if I could
Would I know where I lived
Would I know where I stood
Would I change to a moth
Would I hide in a cloth
Would I wait till I was dry
Would I be a butterfly
Would I live, would I die

Lesley Wilson, 8 years

61 This I ask you, God

Who is God?
What is God?
These are the questions I ask you, Lord.
Why must I breathe to live?
Why must I eat to stay alive?
These are the questions I ask you, Lord.

Why have you let people starve to death?
Have they done you any wrong?
Why do I get ill?
Do I do you ill?

Who are you, God?
Did you really create mankind?
Why must all these things happen?
This I ask you, God.

Barry Kriefman, 12 years

62 Where was God?

And where was God
When war broke out?
Where was he, not to hear them shout?
Where was God when aloud they cried?
Where was God when they died?
Where was God when blood was spilt
Was he asleep
Or was he aware
Or was he fighting the devil?

D. Williamson

63 Waiting

Today or tomorrow I will be here
Waiting
Waiting for something:
An answer,
An answer to all my questions.
So far they've all been lies.
They seem the truth until I discover something new,
Something I was not aware of before.
But maybe there isn't an answer,
I mean, one only,
Because it seems the way you look at it, the answer changes,
The reason changes
And everything is seen in a different light.

Anon, 14 years

64 Indecision

No light to shine and pierce the dark.
No sign or word; just a question mark.
The where and how or who and when,
And mulling it over again and again.
Juggling the options, the schemes and the plans;
Is this divine guidance, or is it just man's?
No clearness of vision; no voice from on high,
Just the same nagging questions, where, when and why.
Should one wait for an answer or go forward in doubt,
Believing in providence, everything will work out?
When you've prayed and waited will then come a voice
Saying, "You are responsible. Go, make your choice."

Gerald Gardiner

65 Answers

Dear Friend,
I remember the time
when I thought I had all the answers.
I was so sure of my knowledge about you.
I read books of great teachings,
listened to fine sermons,
exchanged views of Scripture,
discussed, argued, scorched others
with my enthusiasm.
How necessary it was
to pour all experience of you
into a tight container of words!

All the time, dear Friend,
you smiled and led me on,
over the walls of imagery,
through fences of ideas,
gently showing me that walls and fences
have a rightful place in journey,
that they are there for support and shelter
and that when it's time to move on,
they will be no obstacle to progress.

I am still addicted to words
and I still need to hold you
in ideas and images,
though loosely now, in an open web.
But no longer do I have any answers.
You, dear Friend,
have taken away the questions.

Joy Cowley, from *Aotearoa Psalms*

66 Presence

Expecting Him, my door was open wide:
   Then I looked round
   If any lack of service might be found,
And saw Him at my side:
   How entered, by what secret stair,
   I know not, knowing only He was there.

T.E. Brown

67 The uninvited guest

He seems to come in like the leaves –
Blown in at the open window,
And always on a light and airy day,
Never in stormy weather.
And always, I've noticed,
At an inconvenient time –
Right in the middle of the washing.
He looks at me and shows me these holes in his hands,
And, well, I can see them in his feet.
'Not again,' I say.
'Please don't stand there bleeding
All over the kitchen floor.'

Sometimes he comes softly, sadly,
At night – close, by the side of my bed –
Sometimes I latch the door –

But he never goes away.

Thelma Laycock

PROPHECY AND HOPE

I wish that all the Lord's people were prophets and that the Lord would bestow his spirit on them all!

Numbers 11.29

'Now, Lord my God, you have made your servant king in place of my father David, though I am a mere child, unskilled in leadership. Here I am in the midst of your people, the people of your choice, too many to be numbered or counted. Grant your servant, therefore, a heart with skill to listen, so that he may govern your people justly and distinguish good from evil.'

1 Kings 3.7–9

This word of the Lord came to me: 'Before I formed you in the womb I chose you, and before you were born I consecrated you; I appointed you a prophet to the nations. 'Ah! Lord God,' I answered, 'I am not skilled in speaking; I am too young.' But the Lord said, 'Do not say that you are too young; for you are to go to whatever people I send you, and say whatever I tell you to say. Fear none of them, for I shall be with you to keep you safe.' This was the word of the Lord.

Jeremiah 1.4–8

Take heart among yourselves what you find in Christ Jesus: 'He was in the form of God; yet he laid no claim to equality with God, but made himself nothing, assuming the form of a slave. Bearing the human likeness, sharing the human lot, he humbled himself, and was obedient, even to the point of death, death on a cross! Therefore God raised him to the heights, and bestowed on him the name above all names, that at the name of Jesus every knee should bow – in heaven, on earth, and in the depths – and every tongue acclaim. "Jesus Christ is Lord," to the glory of God the Father.' So you too, my friends, must be obedient.

Philippians 2.5–12

Great and marvellous are your deeds,
O Lord God, sovereign over all;
just and true are your ways,
O King of the ages,
Who shall not fear you, Lord,
and do homage to your name?
For you alone are holy,
All nations shall come and worship before you,
for your just decrees stand revealed.

Revelation 15.3–4

68 Through suffering

When the day comes on which our victory
   will shine like a torch in the night,
   it will be like a dream.
We will laugh and sing for joy.
Then the other nations will say about us,
   'The Lord did great things for them.'
Indeed, he is doing great things for us;
that is why we are happy in our suffering.

Lord, break the chains of humiliation and death,
   just as on that glorious morning
   when you were raised.
Let those who weep
as they sow the seeds of justice and freedom,
gather the harvest of peace and reconciliation.

Those who weep as they go out as instruments of your love
   will come back singing with joy,
   as they will witness the disappearance of hate
and the manifestation of your love in your world.

Zephania Kameeta

69 Come, Lord!

Come,
Lord,
and cover me with the night.
Spread your grace over us
as you assured us you would do.

Your promises are more
than all the stars in the sky;
your mercy is deeper than the night.
Lord,
it will be cold.
The night comes with its breath of death.
Night comes,
the end comes,
but Jesus Christ comes also.
Lord,
we wait for him
day and night.
Amen

A young Ghanaian

70 A day must come

Drinking drop by drop the pure water,
Savouring one by one the sweet fruits, chewing each grain
  of rice,
For how many thousand years:
Sweat, tears, blood, whitened bones,
Is our heritage now and for ever.

Blades of grass, shadows of tree branches,
Dew drops, foam on the water,
Oh, how preciously beautiful, White and pure,
Such is our patrimony,
Our People are wretchedly poor
But with all our native country
Although wretched and stumbling
We would rise up heroically.

Our ancestors have displayed without cease
A boundless life force,
Honours and humiliations, ups and downs, many times in
  the past,
For thousands of years one root remains firm,
The tide recedes to let the wave rise and flow forth,
The trees shed their leaves, numberless buds sprout for life,
Thus tomorrow, a day will come,
It will come: a day must come.

Ngyuen Thai-Binh
a Vietnamese student who was killed trying to hi-jack a plane
to Hanoi as an anti-war protest

71 Hope to live by

I believe that there's
Still hope to live
– not merely to exist.
Somewhere in this
Hopeless whirlpool of life
– a hand extends to help.
In these battered days
You will find, if you search
– one who has offered to mend.
I know that somewhere
In this canyon of despair
– there's a place of relief.
Somewhere in this
Turmoil of confusion
– a right path to follow.
Within this world
Of make-believe
– a faithful friend awaits you.
In this polluted time
We lead
– a hope to be made clean.

Anon

72 More than hope

When winter is around us, we cannot see the spring;
  But still we know,
  Despite the snow,
That spring will come one day.

With night-time's darkness round us, we cannot see the sun;
  But we still know,
  As shadows go,
That dawn will break next day.

When seeds are sown in spring-time, we cannot see the flowers;
  But still we know;
  Prepared below,
A flower will greet the day.

'Though God is all around us, we cannot see his face;
  But still we know;
  Our love says so!
God lives in every day.

Donald Hilton

73 Credo

I believe in one world, full of riches meant for everyone to enjoy;
I believe in one race, the family of mankind,
  learning how to live together by the hard way of self-sacrifice;
I believe in one life, exciting and positive
  which enjoys all beauty, integrity and science;
  uses the discipline of work to enrich society;
  harmonises with the life of Jesus,
  and develops into a total joy.
I believe in one morality, love,
  the holiness of sharing the sorrow and joys of others;
  of bringing together people as true friends;
  of working to get rid of the root causes of poverty and
    injustice, ignorance and fear;
  love, the test of all my thoughts and motives;
  love, guiding me; controlling me; assuring me of God's
    forgiveness;
  and giving me confidence under his Spirit's control.
I believe in Jesus, and the Bible's evidence about him;
  whose life, death and resurrection prove God's lasting
    love for the world;
  who combines in himself life, love, truth, humanity,
    reality and God;
  who saves, guides, and unites all people who follow his way.
I believe in the purpose of God,
  to unite in Christ everything, spiritual or secular;
  to bring about constructive revolution in society,
    individuals and nations;
  and to establish world government under his fatherly direction.

Students of the Indian National Urban Industrial Mission Course

74 In the image of God

I believe that behind the mist the sun waits.
I believe that beyond the dark night it is raining stars.
I believe in secret volcanoes and the world below.
I believe that this lost ship will reach port.
They will not rob me of hope, it shall not be broken . . .
My voice is filled to overflowing
with the desire to sing, the desire to sing.
I believe in reason, and not in the force of arms;
I believe that peace will be sown throughout the earth.
I believe in our nobility, created in the image of God,
and with free will reaching for the skies.
They will not rob me of hope, it shall not be broken,
It shall not be broken.

World Council of Churches 1985 from *Confessing our Faith around the World IV*

75 The people's creed

I believe in a colour blind God,
Maker of technicolour people,
Who created the universe
And provided abundant resources
For equitable distribution among all his people.
I believe in Jesus Christ,
Born of a common woman,
Who was ridiculed, disfigured, and executed,
Who on the third day rose and fought back;
He storms the highest councils of men,
Where he overturns the iron rule of injustice.
From henceforth he shall continue
To judge the hatred and arrogance of men.
I believe in the Spirit of Reconciliation,
The united body of the dispossessed;
The communion of the suffering masses,
The power that overcomes the dehumanising forces of men,
The resurrection of personhood, justice and equality,
And in the final triumph of Brotherhood.

Canaan Banana

76 A common destiny

It matters little where we pass the remnants of our days. A few more moons; a few more winters – and not one of the descendants of the mighty host that once moved over this broad land or lived in happy homes, protected by the Great Spirit, will remain to mourn over the graves of a people once more powerful and hopeful than yours. But why would I mourn at the untimely fate of my people? Tribe follows tribe, and nation follows nation, like the waves of the sea. It is the order of nature. The time of decay may be distant, but it surely comes for everyone. No one is exempt from the common destiny. So, we may be brothers (and sisters) after all. We shall see.

Chief Seathl *on the occasion of surrendering tribal lands*
to the United States government in 1854

77 Freedom

'Well,' he said conclusively, 'however much you pray it doesn't shorten your stretch. You'll sit it out from beginning to end anyhow.'

'Oh, you mustn't pray for that either,' said Aloysha, horrified. 'Why d'you want freedom? In freedom your last grain of faith will be choked with weeds. You should rejoice that you're in prison. Here you have time to think about your soul. As the Apostle Paul wrote: "Why all these tears? Why are you trying to weaken my resolution? For my part I am ready not merely to be bound but even to die for the name of the Lord Jesus." '

Shukov gazed at the ceiling in silence. Now he didn't know either whether he wanted freedom or not. At first he'd longed for it. Every night he'd counted the days of his stretch – how many had passed, how many were coming. And then he'd grown bored with counting. And then it became clear that men of his like wouldn't ever be allowed to return home, that they'd be exiled. And whether his life would be any better there than here – who could tell?

Freedom meant one thing to him – home.

But they wouldn't let him go home.

Alexander Solzhenitsyn
from *One day in the life of Ivan Denisovitch*

78 Dare to love

God made man to be free,
Free within the human family.
The Commonwealth of man is still his dream.
In Charter and in Constitution,
In Petition and in Pact.
He inscribes his faith
In Freedom and Equality.
Yet still the barriers rise
And prejudice is strong.
Fear and suspicion separate
And sever man from man.

Why does the dream delay?
Why is hope unfulfilled?
Man lacks the faith,
He lacks the faith of Christ,
Who lived out his belief,
Who, in a hostile world,
Revealed the potency of love.
By this one act he realised the dream
And bridged the gap that separated man from man.
The wall was down.
And Jew and Gentile,
Slave and free,
Were one in Christ.

So when men dare to love
They can release a power
That heals the sad divisions of mankind.
Where men give up security and home,
To help a backward people with their skills,
There hope is born.
Where statesmen patiently negotiate,
And sacrifice advantage and prestige,
There peace can grow.
Where prisoner kneels before the bullying guard,
Immune to provocation and to hate,
There love can heal.
Where men will venture on a hope
Of truth and goodness yet untried
And take Christ at his word,
There God can work.

Jim Bates

79 Celebration!

Then I saw the earth blazing with sunlight:
I saw children laughing as they learned the secrets of the earth
From people who smiled as they shared their knowledge:
I saw the world celebrating Carnival; black and white,
Protestant and Catholic, Christian and Jew,
All joining hands and dancing through the countryside and
    the city streets:
I saw the streets a mass of colour
Where people left their jobs and houses to join the fun:
And then I saw people returning to jobs
Where they felt the fulfilment of creation:
I saw faces full of peace and joy:
I saw children full of food and excitement:
I saw prisons with open doors for people to come out,
And I saw homes with open doors for people to enter in:
I saw beauty at every street-corner,
And heard music in every home:
I saw people discussing religion in bus-queues,
And politics in the tube:
I saw babies on the knees of old men,
While their parents danced:
I saw green grass, free from litter,
And trees full of birds.
I heard people singing as they cleaned the pavements:
I saw houses, strong and shining with new paint:
I saw each family with a home of their own
And friends to share it.
I saw people free: to love and be loved, to give and to receive.
I saw peace in people's hearts, joy in people's eyes
And a song on everyone's lips:
I saw dreams being dreamt
And lights shining in the darkness:
I saw water in the desert
And fire in the mountains:
I felt warmth in the winter-time
And heard laughter in the rain;
I saw a ten pound-note in the gutter
That nobody had bothered to pick up.

Alison Head

80   Peace is good

When Peace will come, come indeed,
When the dream will finally be true,
When Messiah will come riding on his great white steed,
Solid gold through and through,
And in his hand a banner hold
To show that our expectations have taken place –
Then husband and son, and father old
Need no more danger face
And a little girl will not ask her mother any more,
'But Mommy, who needs war?'
Then in shops they'll sell
Building blocks and every sort of animal,
While in town and village, little boys
Will no more know of guns for toys,
And person to person will smile instead
For Peace is good: I bet you lots!
No more wounded, no more dead,
No more shelters, no more shots;
And where once there was only the bitter sigh,
You will hear singing with spirits high.

Tami Ha'Elyon, 9 years

81   Peace for all

Peace is a young mother
Walking with her son
Hand in hand,
A smile of happiness
On her face:
And you knowing
You will not have
To meet her again in the street
Ten years later
Wearing black,
Tearful and wrinkled
A look of endless grief
In her eyes
Which nothing can console.

Peace is all this
For us and for other people as well.
All this and much,
Much more.

Shai Ben Moshe, 13 years

82 Selecting colours

I had a paint-box –
Each colour glowing with delight;
I had a paint-box with colours
Warm and cool and bright.
I had no red for wounds and blood,
I had no black for an orphaned child,
I had no white for the face of the dead,
I had no yellow for burning sands.
I had orange for joy and life,
I had green for buds and blooms,
I had blue for clear bright skies,
I had pink for dreams and rest.
I sat down
and painted
Peace.

Tali Shurek, 13 years

83 I don't like wars

I don't like wars
They end up with monuments;
I don't want battles to roar
Even in neighbouring continents.

I like Spring
Flowers producing,
Fields covered with green,
The wind in the hills whistling.

Drops of dew I love,
The scent of jasmine as night cools,
Stars in darkness above,
And rain singing in pools.

I don't like wars. They end
In wreaths and monuments;
I like Peace come to stay
And it will some day.

Matti Yosef, 9 years

84 Solidarity

Let us open the clenched fist and extend the open palms
Let us mourn till others are comforted, weep till others laugh
Let us be sleepless till all can sleep untroubled
Let us be meek till all can stand up in pride
Let us be frugal till all are filled
Let us give till all have received
Let us make no claims till all have had their due
Let us be slaves till all are free
Let us lay down our lives till others have life abundantly.

John Harriott

85 Warp and weft

Peace is like gossamer –
vulnerable, yet indestructible:
tear it, and it will be rewoven.
Peace does not despair.
Begin to weave a web of peace:
start in the centre
and make peace with yourself
and your God.
Take the threads outwards
and build peace within your family, your community
– and in the circle of those you find it hard to like.
Then stretch your concern
into all the world.
Weave a web of peace
and do not despair.
Love is the warp in the fabric of life:
truth is the weft:
care and integrity together –
vulnerable,
but ultimately
indestructible.
Together,
they spell
peace . . .

Kate Compston

86 A Litany for the Day of Human Rights

For those who grasp their prison bars helplessly
    so that we may walk free – a thought.
For those who rot in the dark
    so that we may walk in the sun – a thought.
For those whose ribs have been broken
    so that we may breathe our fill – a thought.
For those whose faces have been slapped
    so that we may walk in fear of no hand – a thought.
For those whose mouths have been gagged
    so that we may speak out – a thought.
For those whose wives live in anguish
    so that our wives may live happy – a thought.
For those whose country is in chains
    so that our country may be free – a thought.
And for the jailers and for their torturers
    – a thought.
    The saddest of all, they are the most maimed,
    and the day of reckoning is bound to come.

Salvador de Madariaga

87 Against domination

During my lifetime I have dedicated myself to the struggle of the
African people. I have fought against white domination, and I have
fought against black domination. I have cherished the ideal of a
democratic and free society in which all persons live together in
harmony with equal opportunities. It is an ideal which I hope
to live for and to achieve. But, if needs be, it is an ideal for which
I am prepared to die.

Nelson Mandela
from his speech before sentence was passed on him in the Riviona trial in 1963

88 Christmas thanksgiving

Thank God . . .
for empty churches
and bursting shops;
for the soldier's Christmas Eve patrol;
for starvation
and gluttony;
for recklessly randy playboys;
for tenements
and prisons;
for apartheid-cheapened oranges;
for boring sermons
and trivial TV;
for minds warped by bent schooling;
for drunks
and thugs;
for wreaths made out of holly;
for mucked-up sex
and prudery;
for comfortable affluence;
for ignorance
and selfishness;
for foreigners in foreign lands;
for missiles
and war toys;
for hymns that can't be understood;
for me
and mine.

Thank God for these
else we would soon forget
the world to which Christ came
(and why)
and lose the meaning
in the cosy celebration.

David J. Harding

89   Be honest!

Be honest about violence . . .
how it thrills the blood,
enables men
to stand erect and act,
to exercise such power
and savage force
that rescues from
the cowardly and the trite.

Be honest about violence . . .
how it spills the blood
and tears through flesh
and nerve and bone and life,
destroying the better sorts of power
and ways of life
and hurting most
the civilised and weak.

Be honest about violence . . .
how sometimes it helps
the victor and his victory;
and on occasion has been known
to help the victim too.
Be honest. Let
the victim judge . . . for once!

David J. Harding

SONGS OF JOY AND SADNESS

I shall bless the Lord at all times;
his praise will be ever on my lips.
In the Lord I shall glory;
the humble will hear and be glad.
Glorify the Lord with me;
let us exalt his name together.

Psalm 34.1–3

Save me, God
for the water has risen to my neck.
I sink in muddy depths where there is no foothold;
I have come into deep water, and the flood sweeps me away.
I am exhausted with crying, my throat is sore,
my eyes are worn out with waiting for God.

Psalm 69.1–3

My soul tells out the greatness of the Lord,
my spirit has rejoiced in God my Saviour;
for he has looked with favour on his servant,
lowly as she is.
From this day forward all generations will count me blessed,
for the Mighty God has done great things for me.

Luke 1.46–49

Will the Lord always reject me
and never again show favour?
Has his love now failed utterly?
Will his promise never be fulfilled?
Has God forgotten to be gracious?
Has he in anger withheld his compassion?
Has his right arm grown weak? I said.
Has the right hand of the Most High changed?

Psalm 77.7–10

Awake, sleeper,
rise from the dead,
and Christ will shine upon you.

Ephesians 5.14

90 I fly!

You big, bright, beautiful God,
this is my day for flying!
I reach out to the bigness of you.
I touch the brightness of you
and I feel the beauty of you
in the centre of my living.
Today you bear me up, up,
past my doubts about both of us,
to the certainty of your love.

Today, God, I know you.
All those words I learned
are burnt up in your fire.
You are sun to my Icarus,
candle to my moth.
Today I fly
and am dissolved in you!

And if tomorrow I am grounded
by a weight of anxieties,
if my feet are heavy and there are clouds
between me and the sun,
then let me keep hold
of the warm place in my heart
reminding me that today I flew
and was kissed by God.

Joy Cowley, from *Aotearoa Psalms*

91   A psalm of praise

Praise the Lord all flowers and trees,
Sing his praises wasps and bees.

Daffodils and small primroses,
Show your thanks in groups and poses.

Skip and hop you baby rabbit,
Make his praise your daily habit.

Worship him you clouds and fogs,
Wag your tails you happy dogs.

Dig for joy all moles and worms,
And worship him in happy terms.

Come forth from your cosy lair,
And join the throng, O little bear.

Praise the Lord, O night and day,
The moon's pale light and sun's bright ray.

Shout his praises, old and young,
Keep thanks and praises on your tongue.

Lift up your voices large and small;
Sing praise to him who made us all.

Mary Wakelin, 10 years

92   A circle of praise

Now is the time to live,
to come to the Father who creates us,
to sing to the Lord who frees us,
to dance with the Spirit who fills us.

Let us invite the city
to worship with us.

We call the traffic in the streets,
department stores,
revolving doors,
and all the people
in the yellow pages,
to stop and shout his name.

Let us invite our leaders
to glorify his name.

We summon doctor, politician, star,
president, professor, clown,
to step down
and kneel with us.

Let us invite the injured people
to speak with us.

We ask all people, living alone,
the blacks and the whites
who have no rights,
the unemployed and angry poor,
to tell the truth in love.

Let us extend an open invitation
to one and all
to join in one full circle of joy.

Join the circle, Lord,
and make our joy complete.

Norman C. Habel (adapted)

93 Praise

I've been looking for a suitable word
to praise you, Lord. Something enthusiastic
but not too formal, the sort of happy shout
a child gives to its mother.
I've tried Hallelujahs, Glorias and Hosannas,
but really, what I'd like is a word
from my own language, a word that is me.
If I were a bellbird, I'd fill my throat
with ecstatic song. Or, as a lamb,
I could fling myself into a spring dance.
As a mountain stream I would spill out
inarticulate babblings of joy.
And if I were the sea, my waves would explode
in a thunder of love for you.
Lord, you overwhelm me with your great goodness.
Praise should not be difficult and yet
I can't find the exact word. Perhaps
it doesn't exist, though if it does,
I'm sure that it sounds like "Yippee!"

Joy Cowley, from *Aotearoa Psalms*

94 High flight

Oh I have slipped the surly bonds of earth,
And danced the skies on laughter-silvered wings;
Sunward I've climbed and joined the tumbling mirth
Of sunsplit clouds, and done a hundred things
        you have not dreamed of.

Soared and wheeled and swung,
High in the sunlit silence hovering there,
I've chased the shouting winds along
And flung my eager craft through footless halls of air.

Up, up, the long delirious burning blue,
I've topped the windswept heights with easy grace
Where never lark or even eagle flew.

And as with silent lifted mind, I've trod
The high, untrespassed sanctity of space,
Put out my hand, and touched the face of God.

J.G. Magee,
A second world war fighter pilot killed on his first mission

95 Jesus Christ is Lord!

Christ is the Lord of the smallest atom,
Christ is the Lord of outer space,
Christ is the Lord of the constellations,
Christ is the Lord of every place;

Of the furthest star,
Of the coffee bar,
Of every dividing wall;
Of the village green,
Of the Asian scene,
Christ is the Lord of all;

Christ is the Lord of the human heart-beat,
Christ is the Lord of every breath,
Christ is the Lord of man's existence,
Christ is the Lord of life and death.

Christ is the Lord of our thoughts and feelings,
Christ is the Lord of all we plan,
Christ is the Lord of a man's decision,
Christ is the Lord of a total man:

In the local street,
Where the people meet,
In the church or the nearby hall;
In the factory,
In the family,
Christ is the Lord of all.

Christ is the Lord of our love and courtship,
Christ is the Lord of man and wife,
Christ is the Lord of the things we care for,
Christ is the Lord of all our life.

Anon

96 Fit for God

Holy God, who madest me
And all things else to worship Thee;
Keep me fit in mind and heart,
Body and soul to take my part.
Fit to stand, fit to run,
Fit for sorrow, fit for fun,
Fit to work and fit to play,
Fit to face life day by day:
Holy God, who madest me,
Make me fit to worship Thee.

Anon

97 Joints in praise

O you shoulders, elbows, wrists,
  bless him, praise him, magnify him for ever;
you fittings of thumbs and fingers,
  bless ye the Lord;
hips, thighs, spine in its multiples,
  bless him, praise him, magnify him for ever.

Charles Williams

98 At the end of the day

The long day has worn out my body.
I give thanks
that I was able to work hard
for a good cause –
and that I earned some money.

Thanks,
Lord,
that I could use my voice,
my shoulders,
my arms,
my hands.

Lord,
I am tired,
I am falling asleep,
Hallelujah for this day!

A young Ghanaian

99 Joy

And joy is everywhere; it is in the earth's green covering of grass; in the blue serenity of the sky; in the reckless exuberance of spring; in the severe abstinence of grey winter; in the living flesh that animates our bodily frame; in the perfect poise of the human figure, noble and upright; in living; in the exercise of all our powers; in the acquisition of knowledge; in fighting evils; in dying for gains we never can share. Joy is there everwhere; it is superfluous, unnecessary; nay, it very often contradicts the most peremptory behests of necessity. It exists to show that the bonds of law can only be explained by love; they are like body and soul. Joy is the realisation of the truth of oneness, the oneness of our soul with the world and of the world-soul with the supreme lover.

Rabindranath Tagore, from *Sadhana*

100 Monday 24 May 1875

This afternoon I walked over to Lanhill. As I came down from the hill into the valley across the golden meadows and among the flower-scented hedges a great wave of emotion and happiness stirred and rose up within me. I know not why I was so happy, nor what I was expecting, but I was in a delirium of joy; it was one of the supreme few moments of existence, a deep delicious draught from the strong sweet cup of life. It came unsought, unbidden, at the meadow stile, it was one of the flowers of happiness scattered for us and found unexpectedly by the wayside of life. It came silently, suddenly, and it went as it came, but it left a long lingering glow and glory behind as it faded slowly like a gorgeous sunset, and I shall ever remember the place and the time in which such great happiness fell upon me.

Francis Kilvert, from *Francis Kilvert's Diary*

101 Rainbow's Delight

My heart leaps up when I behold
  A rainbow in the sky:
So was it when my life began;
So is it now I am a man:
So be it when I shall grow old,
  Or let me die!
The child is father of the man;
And I could wish my days to be
Bound each to each by natural piety.

William Wordsworth

102 Sky songs

I have thrilled to the notes of a blackbird's song,
  The moorland curlew's cry,
A lark's long throbbing ecstasy
  Flooding the summer sky.
But the call that stirs my heart,
  And sets my eyes alight,
Is the wild call, the haunting call,
  Of gulls in soaring flight.

For it calls me afar to the towering cliffs,
  And rocks where the great seas break;
To islands lost in summer haze,
  Ships with a foaming wake:
Where the gulls in grey and white,
  Upborne on tireless wing,
With a wild cry, a haunting cry,
  In ceaseless circles swing.

Albert F. Bayly

103 Sonnet

When God created Adam out of clay
Placing him east of Eden long ago,
He little thought what kind of race would grow
To shame the man he moulded on that day,
But took the rib while sleeping Adam lay
As if he were determined we should know
The truth his son would live and die to show,
Though from the first we could not keep God's way.
Better for all if he had stayed his hand,
Leaving the beasts as keepers of his land;
Through ages men have fought with upward gaze,
Tributes of blood to deities unknown,
Confused by hearts that hold a need to praise
With minds that mock simplicity outgrown.

Margaret Portch, 17 years

104 Hope through pain

Young as I am, life is so cruel
nothing in life seems to work out well
I have counted my days with hurt and long sufferings
my months and years are well full of labouring.

Life is uneasy, friends are full of untruths
lovers are spiteful, treacherous and deadly
every day as it wanes leaves me disillusioned
I wonder if such will be my lifelight.

In dreams and in visions life is so gay-good
my horoscope predicts some brighter futures
but all my hopes and trusts end in ruptures
amidst men's deeds of hurt I go astray . . .

Still on-on I'll strive and struggle
someday, somehow I know my world will settle
for life-lived is like the storms of the seas
sometimes it storms, sometimes subsides . . .

Pat Amadu Maddy

105 Sitting

Here I am, sitting on the wall
waiting for a job.
I count the men,
sitting nearby
waiting for work.
Lord, can't you do something
so that there is more work
and the bosses are more just?
One grows lazy
sitting around.
One gets used to it.
And it hurts me
that once again
I can take nothing home
to my children and wife.
But I will not complain.
I know
you have everything in your hand.

And, just across the street
you let everything grow
so that at least we do not go hungry.
You are a merciful and good God.
What are these wood and clay gods
beside you?
You are the greatest,
and you do as you will.
And that is good for all.
Amen.

Anon

106 Complaint

Damn You, God,
For setting things up like this,
For the pain of loss,
Gradual, long drawn-out
Of all that makes life good to live,
And for the pain of watching it happen
To someone you love.
For the anger and the guilt
The breaking up
The helplessness
For making things like this.

Don't tell me that it's all our fault,
Our own most miserable fault.
Some of it is.
But not all, Lord.
Not all.

W.S. Beattie

107 Lullaby

hush my little baby
rest:
there's not much milk
left in my breast
there's not much milk
left in the world
that's why we starve
– for kindness –

hush my little baby
rest:
we'll wait here, soon
– perhaps it's best –
we'll not see the grey day dawning

Anon

108 Fury

I am furious.
Furious with you,
furious with me,
furious with everyone.

Nobody cares,
or gives to you,
or gives to me,
or gives a toss.

They are all dying
to have life,
to have love,
to have you.

Why not show them
who you are,
who I am,
who they are?

I am furious.
Nobody cares,
and I'm dying
to show them you.

Melanie Smith

109 Lost: a prayer in the void

The wind moans
The rain sobs
But the heavens are not weeping for me.
I love him
But he loves her
  The simplest situation ever to be.

Sunday
It's Sunday
Distantly the church bells are ringing
Songs of praise
On the air
Windy gusts of fervent hymn singing.

Where are the hills
from whence cometh my help?
There is only a plain
A flat desert of despair
I have never been so alone
There is nothing at all out there.

Anon, 17 years

110 Not by bread alone

You promised me my life; but you lied. You think that life is nothing but not being stone dead. It is not the bread and water I fear. I can live on bread: when have I asked for more? It is no hardship to drink water if the water be clean. . . . But to shut me from the sight of the fields and flowers; to chain my feet so that I can never again ride with the soldiers nor climb the hills; to make me breathe foul damp darkness, and keep me from everything that brings me back to the love of God . . . all this is worse than the furnace in the bible that was heated seven times. I could do without my warhorse; I could drag about in a skirt; I could let the banners and the trumpets and the knights and soldiers pass me and leave me behind as they leave the other women, if only I could still hear the wind in the trees, the larks in the sunshine, the young lambs crying through the healthy frost, and the blessed blessed church bells that send my angel voices floating to me on the wind. But without these things I cannot live . . .

George Bernard Shaw, from *St. Joan*

St. Joan was to be burnt at the stake as a heretic but she recanted and so was saved, only to be told she would be imprisoned for life. The speech above shows the kind of answer she gave.

111 It is not good

It is not good
To watch an old man die;
A high domed forehead, fringed with silver silk,
Transparent ivory ears,
That hear no more,
A sharp beaked nose, networked with thin red skeins
Above a drooped moustache,
And bloodless lips, brown scummed,
Mumbling to long dead friends,
While scrawny throat
Flutters like captive bird
And alabaster fingers, nails too clean,
Fumble the starched sheet.

Around the ward, each in his captive bed,
Lie waxwork figures, graven, listless, mute,
White haired and open mouthed,
Blank-eyed and still.
By each bedside table, water glass,
An orange or an apple,
Grapes or flowers,
Gifts from the living to the dying dead.

On stools by each the waiting relatives,
A yard away but separate
By gulf unbridgeable,
Sit in a world of sterile cleanness,
Groping for words to speak,
The world of life confronting world of death.

Outside the streets are wet,
The traffic roars;
The living hurry by, intent on life,
Unmindful of the room
Where old men lie
Awaiting death.
It is not good to watch an old man die.

S. Clafton, 14 years

112 A closed church

Silent the bell, it tolls no more.
The Church is just a shell, closed is the door,
Closed by people with common sense,
cold indifference, lack of pence.
A lone silhouette on a bleak Pennine top.
Do they ever pause and stop
to think of the Church in its prime,
Christmas – Easter and Harvest time?
Often have I climbed those meadows steep,
when Winter snow lay white, deep,
to sing my praise of Saviour's birth,
'Goodwill to men, Peace on Earth'.
The lark soars high his song to sing,
to welcome yet another Spring.
The soft wind whispers in the grass,
another hill another cross.
Beneath granite, stone and earthen mound,
deep within that hallowed ground,
lie Father, Mother, Sister, Friend.
What to them this permissive, modern trend?
Have we betrayed their loving trust,
will there again blossom from the dust
a brave new church proudly planned?
If not, I pray they will understand.

Anon

GOOD NEWS

After John had been arrested, Jesus came into Galilee proclaiming the gospel of God: 'The time has arrived; the kingdom of God is upon you. Repent, and believe the gospel.

Mark 1.14–15

Men of Israel, hear me: I am speaking of Jesus of Nazareth, singled out by God and made known to you through miracles, portents and signs, which God worked among you through him, as you well know. By the deliberate will and plan of God he was given into your power, and you killed him, using heathen men to crucify him. But God raised him to life again, setting him free from the pangs of death, because it could not be that death should keep him in its grip.

Acts 2.22–24

To prove that you are sons, God has sent into our hearts the Spirit of his Son, crying, 'Abba, Father!' You are therefore no longer a slave but a son, and if a son, an heir by God's own act.

Galatians 4.6–7

'I have spoken thus to you, so that my joy may be in you, and your joy complete. This is my commandment: love one another as I have loved you. There is no greater love than this, that someone should lay down his life for his friends. You are my friends, if you do what I command you. No longer do I call you servant, for a servant does not know what his master is about. I have called you friends, because I have disclosed to you everything I heard from my Father. You did not choose me: I chose you. I appointed you to go on and bear fruit, fruit that will last; so that the Father may give you whatever you ask in my name. This is my commandment to you: love one another.

John 15.11–17

113 Rumours of God

We have heard about you,
God of all power.
You made the world out of kindness,
creating order out of confusion;
you made each one of us in your own image;
your fingerprint is on every soul.
So we praise you.
We praise and worship you.

We have heard about you,
Jesus Christ:
the carpenter who left his tools and trade;
the poor man who made others rich;
the healer who let himself be wounded;
the criminal on whom the soldiers spat
not knowing they were fouling the face of God;
the saviour who died and rose again.
So we praise you.
We praise and worship you.

We have heard about you,
Holy Spirit.
You broke the bonds of every race and nation,
to let God speak in every tongue;
you made disciples drunk with grace;
you converted souls and emptied pockets;
you showed how love made all things new
and opened the doors to change and freedom.
So we praise you.
We praise and worship you.

Wild Goose Worship Group, from *A Wee Worship Book*

114 Advent longing

These are the greedy days.
It used to be
That Advent was a longing fast,
A time to feel our need
In faith and tingling hope
And keen-eyed looking forward.
Now we cannot wait
But day by day and week by week
We celebrate obsessively
Clutching at Christmas.
When at last it comes,
The day itself,
Our glass is empty.
We have held the feast
Already, and the news is stale
Before it ever reaches us.
We cheat ourselves.
Yet – somehow – still we hope
In these spoiled days
That there may be a child.

W.S. Beattie

115 John 3.16

In the light of evolution and the revelation of depth-
psychological insights the new lines of the Christ-myth will
assume a form something like this: God so loved the world
that he implanted deep within matter itself the promise of
the Christ-life, to the end that in the course of continuing
creation through evolution it would one day flower in Jesus of
Nazareth, thereby quickening the same Christ-life in others to
the eventual rise of the new man on earth.

John Yungblut

116 Cradled

The circle of a girl's arms
have changed the world
the round and sorrowful world
to a cradle for God.

She has laid love in his cradle.
In every cot,
Mary has laid her child.

In each
comes Christ.
In each Christ comes
to birth,
comes Christ from the Mother's breast,
as the bird from the sun
returning,
returning again to the tree he knows
and the nest,
to last year's rifled nest.

Into our hands
Mary has given her child,
heir to the world's tears,
heir to the world's toil,
heir to the world's scars,
heir to the chill dawn
over the ruin of wars.

She has laid love in his cradle,
answering for us all.
'Be it done unto me.'

Caryll Houselander

117 Birth of a King

Did you see Mary counting the cobwebs
On the stable walls, waiting,
In her fullness, for the time
When she would cry out
Among the straw bales while the
Cattle watched her labour?
That was the birth of a king
That I watch through the glittering
Of a star on my carol sheet.
Did you see the shepherds as they
Stumbled from the snow on the hills
With numb fingers and the filth
Of old sheep under their nails?
Did you see the crown fall
From the head of a king
As he wandered from the warmth
Of his palace into an ice-sodden world
Waiting for summer? There they stand
With their boxes and pout for the Christmas cards.
I wonder how many times they had to
Stop because they had lost the star?

Kaye Tompkins, 17 years

118 To Jesus on his birthday

For this your Mother sweated in the cold;
For this you bled upon the bitter tree:
A yard of tinsel ribbon bought and sold,
A paper wreath, a day at home for me.
The merry bells ring out: the people kneel:
Up goes the man of God before the crowd;
With voice of honey, and with eyes of steel,
He drones your humble gospel to the proud.
Nobody listens. Less than the wind that blows
Are all your words to us you died to save.
O, Prince of Peace! O, Sharon's dewy rose!
How mute you lie within your vaulted grave.
The stone the angel rolled away with tears
Is back upon your mouth these thousand years.

Edna St Vincent Millay

119 The wonderful night

The moon was glowing softly
I hummed a little tune
I sat upon a crumpled rock
Hungry silent and cold
We huddled together like children
Trying to keep warm
The sheep baaing softly
I looked up to the gloomy sky
And saw a strange light
Getting closer and closer
I put my hands above my head so
as it would not blind me
I knocked against the others we were
all scared
What could it be?
Angels were singing so beautiful and
said
Go to Bethlehem where a blessed Baby lies
We took a lamb each
We had nothing else to give
We crept in quietly so as not to disturb him
But he was awake and giggling so sweetly
Mary had wrapped him in swaddling.

Fiona Bonnar, 8 years

120 The burning Babe

As I in hoary winter's night stood shivering in the snow,
Surprised I was with sudden heat which made my heart to glow;
And lifting up a fearful eye to view what fire was near,
A pretty Babe all burning bright did in the air appear;
Who, scorched with excessive heat, such floods of tears did shed,
As though his floods should quench his flames which with
    his tears were fed.
'Alas!' quoth he, 'but newly born in fiery heats I fry,
Yet none approach to warm their hearts or feel my fire but I.
My faultless breast the furnace is, the fuel wounding thorns;
Love is the fire, and sighs the smoke, the ashes shame and scorns;
The fuel justice layeth on, and mercy blows the coals;
The metal in this furnace wrought are men's defiled souls:
For which, as now on fire I am to work them to their good,
So I will melt into a bath to wash them in my blood.'
With this he vanished out of sight and swiftly shrunk away,
And straight I called unto mind that it was Christmas-day.

Robert Southwell

121 Shapes of Christ

God abides in men
because Christ has put on
the nature of man, like a garment,
and worn it to His own shape.
He has put on everyone's life.
He has fitted Himself to the little child's dress,
to the shepherd's coat of sheepskin,
to the workman's coat,
to the king's red robes,
to the snowy loveliness of the wedding garment,
and to the drab
of the sad simple battle-dress.
He has given man His crown,
and thorn that is jewelled
with drops of His blood.
He has fastened His hands
to the tree of life.
He has latched His feet
in crimson sandals,
that they move not
from the path of love.
God abides in man.

Caryll Houselander

122 Evolution towards Christ

There are not two separate and distinct natures in Jesus, the divine and the human, as the Church has maintained since the final articulation of the concept at the Council of Chalcedon in 451. The modern depth-psychological perception of the inviolable psychosomatic unity of human personality will not allow such a dichotomy. There was only one nature – the human – but this was shot through with the divine element which consists of what man has it in him to become, the new man, the second Adam, the son of man. Human nature is itself evolving, realising gradually more of its divine potential.

John Yungblut

123 Black Christmas

Well, that's a washout.
God knows where the party was,
But somewhere else.
It figures.
Sit in the car and wonder what to do
(Is there anything to do?)
Near the darkened church where last night
We sang carols,
And also in the morning.
But in the afternoon,
Just for a change,
We went and sang them somewhere else.
Tomorrow
And the next day
And Christmas Day itself
There'll be the chance to sing some more.
You get sick of bloody carols.

What's the use of sitting here,
I might as well go home
And let my mother talk to me again.
God! Five more bloody days.
I suppose carols are better than nothing,
Some kind of way
To be with other people
In an impersonal benevolent togetherness.
Only they will keep on
About rejoicing.
Maybe it's OK for them.
Perhaps they dwell perpetually in felicity.
Perhaps.
Oh come on, start the car,
Get going
Somewhere.
But what's the use,
I take myself
Along with me.

Anon

124 A Dissenter's Hail Mary

You bore him, fed him, clothed him, led him;
You nursed him, enfolded him, encouraged him, scolded him;
You suffered him, moved him to laugh (and to weep).
You were the chosen one, you were the maiden,
He was yours before he was ours;
With your flesh the Word was laden,
Seed of eternity, Hope of the years.
For your obedience, your faith and your firmness,
For your humility, tenderness, grace,
Sinners salute you: presume to say 'Thank you',
Who love him and would serve him
    But had not your place.

James Badcock

125 Declining shadow

The shadow of his later cross
Falls over Bethlem's town.
The barren stable is a sign,
His star is in decline!
Yet richness shines in poverty,
True kingship needs no crown,
The Son of Man is dispossessed:
Humility's renown.

Near Calvary's hill King Herod plots;
The child must surely die!
Fierce soldiers search the wintry streets
To see where infants lie.
The holy family flees the night,
Rejection makes a start.
For Mary, thirty years from now,
The sword will pierce her heart.

The shadow of his later cross
Falls over Bethlem's town.
The barren stable is a sign,
His star is in decline!
Yet in the pain of manger-cross
Is life and hope for me,
For Christ brought low in stable bare
Reigns for eternity.

Donald Hilton

126 Jesus the obscure

There are people after Jesus.
They have seen the signs.
Quick, let's hide him.
Let's think; carpenter,
    fisherman's friend,
    disturber of religious comfort.
Let's award him a degree in theology,
a purple cassock
and a position of respect.
They'll never think of looking here.
Let's think;
his dialect may betray him,
his tongue is of the masses.
Let's teach him Latin
and seventeenth century English,
they'll never think of listening in.
Let's think;
humble,
Man of Sorrows,
nowhere to lay his head.
We'll build a house for him,
somewhere away from the poor.
We'll fill it with brass and silence.
It's sure to throw them off.

There are people after Jesus.
Quick, let's hide him.

Steve Turner

127 Jesus the unconventional

What happened to me as the work (of translating the New Testament) progressed was that the figure of Jesus emerged more and more clearly, and in a way unexpectedly. Or course I had deep respect, indeed a great reverence, for the conventional Jesus Christ whom the Church worshipped. But I was not at all prepared for the unconventional man revealed in these terse Gospels. No one could possibly have invented such a person: this was no puppet-hero built out of the imaginations of adoring admirers. 'This man

Jesus' so briefly described, rang true, sometimes alarmingly true. I began to see now why the religious Establishment of those days wanted to get rid of him at all costs. He was sudden death to pride, pomposity and pretence . . .

The record of the behaviour of Jesus on the way to the cross and of the crucifixion itself is almost unbearable, chiefly because it is so intensely human. If, as I believe, this was indeed God focused in a human being, we can see for ourselves that here is no play-acting, this is the real thing. There are no supernatural advantages for this man. No celestial rescue party delivered him from the power of evil men, and his agony was not mitigated by any superhuman anaesthetic. We can only guess what frightful anguish of mind and spirit wrung from him the terrible words, 'My God, my God, why hast thou forsaken me?' But the cry 'It is finished!' cannot be one of despair. It does not even mean 'It is all over!' It means 'It has been completed' – and the terrifying task of doing God's will to the bitter end had been fully and finally accomplished.

J.B. Phillips, from *Ring of Truth*

128 Jesus recognised

Here is a man who was born in an obscure village, the child of a peasant woman. He worked in a carpenter's shop until he was thirty, and then for three years he was an itinerant preacher. He had no credentials but himself. While still a young man, the tide of popular opinion turned against him. His friends – the twelve men who had learned so much from him, and had promised him their enduring loyalty – ran away, and left him. He went through a mockery of a trial; he was nailed upon a cross between two thieves; when he was dead, he was taken down and laid in a borrowed grave through the pity of a friend.

Yet I am well within the mark when I say that all the armies that ever marched, and all the parliaments that ever sat, and all the kings that ever reigned, put together, have not affected the life of man upon this earth as has this one solitary life.

Anon

129 A man for all seasons

What is meant when we say that we must be 'like Jesus'? It may be that most people tend to find in Jesus (if they look at him at all) a vindication of a life-style which they have already chosen for themselves for other reasons. If you are a priest you see in Jesus the epitome of the great High Priest. If you are a layman Jesus does not look like a priest at all. He is seen as the most lay of all great spiritual leaders. If you are a radical, you take your inspiration from the Jesus who came to turn the world upside down. If you are a conservative, you rejoice that Jesus said that not one jot or tittle of tradition would be altered. If you are a quiet man, you see in Jesus the one who was always withdrawing into a desert place for peace and meditation. If you are a man of action, Jesus is seen as the dynamic leader who was always to be found in the thick of every conflict. If you are a pacifist, Jesus is on your side because he urged his followers to turn the other cheek. If you are a militarist, you are glad he drove the corrupt traders from the temple with a scourge of cords. If you are a lover of good things, Jesus is your man. He was often criticised because he was a friend of wine imbibers and harlots. If you are a Puritan at heart, you are glad to follow the one who set so little store by worldly pleasures that he had nowhere to lay his head.

It is a matter of paying your money and taking your choice? Or is it really because Jesus was a man for all seasons?

Edward Patey, from *Christian Life Style*

130 Asking for trouble?

Excitement grew to fever pitch,
The army drafted to the town,
Authority must be maintained
And troublemakers be put down.

The city's full to bursting point,
Informers mingle with the crowd.
Peace must be kept at any price,
No demonstrations are allowed.

Now church and state for once agree,
Arrest all suspects without charge!
The individual doesn't count
When vested interests are so large.

He could have stayed in Galilee.
He could have walked unnoticed by.
Instead he rode, the King of Kings!
Hosanna! Demonstrator, die!

Ruth Connolly

131 The church's memory

The church — every gathering of the church, everywhere, under every form — *remembers* that on a certain night its Founder said and did certain definite things, briefly reported; that on the same night he fell into the hands of his enemies; and that he suffered a violent death (for the broken body and the shed blood can mean nothing else). The memory of the church thus takes us back to the same point where we formerly dropped anchor on our journey up the stream of history — the moment of the foundation of the church, when its Founder 'suffered under Pontius Pilate'. All lines run back to that precise point, which we might date tentatively to Friday April 7, AD30. Not indeed that the exact calendar date is either certain or important; other dates are possible between AD29 and 33, but it *is* of some importance that the church remembers an event which is actual, concrete and in principle dateable like any other historical event.

The remembrance goes back in a continuous chain. At every service there are present elderly people who fifty or sixty years ago heard those words spoken by, or in the presence of, men old enough to be their grandparents; there are young people who, it may be, will repeat them in the hearing of their grandchildren. And so the endless chain goes on. For nineteen centuries there has not been one single week in which this act of remembrance was not made, one generation reminding another.

C.H. Dodd, from *The Founder of Christianity*

132 Bread, wine and gentleness

Be gentle
When you
touch bread.
Let it not lie
uncared for,
unwanted:
So often bread
Is taken for granted.
There is such beauty
In bread,
Beauty of sun and soil,
Beauty of patient toil.
Wind and rain have caressed it,
Christ often blessed it.
Be gentle
When you touch bread.

Be loving
When you
drink wine.
So freely received
and joyfully shared
In the spirit of him
who cared.
Warm as a flowing river,
Shining and clear
As the sun.
Deep as the soil
Of human toil.
The winds and rain caressed it.
Christ often blessed it.
Be loving
when you drink wine.

Anon

133 Three tables

Each family
At table meets;
From home and school
Each other greet:
A time to talk,
A time to eat,
Welcome and love
Each day repeat.

Some tables full;
Some sadly bare:
To sacrifice
Who now will dare?
Then, giving thanks,
Begin to share,
Since Christ the Lord
Invites our care.

We gather round
A table here.
We meet as friends,
The Lord is near.
With bread and wine
We celebrate:
By sign and word
Christ's love relate.

Donald Hilton

134 Only a house

What is this place where we are meeting?
Only a house, the earth its floor,
walls and a roof, sheltering people,
windows for light, an open door.
Yet it becomes a body that lives
when we are gathered here
and know our God is near.

Words from afar, stars that are falling,
sparks that are sown in us like seed,
names for our God, dreams, signs and wonders
sent from the past are all we need.
We in this place remember and speak
again what we have heard:
God's free redeeming word.

And we accept bread at his table,
broken and shared, a living sign.
Here in this world, dying and living,
we are each others' bread and wine.
This is the place where we can receive
what we need to increase
God's justice and his peace.

Huub Oosterhuis

135 Nail

Nail
Cool, steel, nail,
Hands
Soft, warm hands,
Nail
Cool, steel, nail,
Feet
Soft, warm feet
On the wooden cross,
His body pinned.
Drugged wine offered,
Refused.
Darkness,
silence,
Noon to three.
No natural darkness
No normal eclipse.
'My God, my God, why hast thou forsaken me?'
The wooden cross pieces silhouetted,
Against the dark sky.
Pain and agony,
Inflicted by nails.
'Let us see if Elijah will save him now,'
The scorning watchers shout.
'Father, forgive them, they know not
   what they do.'
He bowed his head
Hair damp with sweat,
And died.
Nails,
Cool, steel nails,
Limbs,
Cold, hard limbs.

John L. Truelove, 16 years

136 Living on in love

Christ on the cross,
Not crushed by death,
But broken by his love too deep for knowing;
Christ on the cross,
Not crushed by death,
But living on in love too deep for crushing.

Christ on the cross,
Not slain for sin,
But broken by his love too great for giving;
Christ on the cross
Not crushed by death,
But living on in love too great for slaying.

Christ on the cross,
Not killed by man,
But broken by his love too strong for holding;
Christ on the cross,
Not crushed by death,
But living on in love too strong for killing.

Clare Richards

137 Is it possible?

is it possible
for a man to speak
to another man's heart?
for a man on
a cross
2000 years
upon a hill
to speak
today to
a man's own
heart?
is it possible
for one man's
death
to be another
man's life
when that man's
death
2000 years
upon a hill
said death
to his friends
and desolation
to his mother?
is it possible
for one man's
shadow to
throw light
on life and love
2000 years

is it?

Anon

25

138 Easter

It is by sinning
That we bind ourselves
Upon the cross
In pain
To expiate the suffering that we cause
If it be possible.

It is the love
Against which we offend
That nails us there
To feel, in helplessness,
The hurt that we have done.

It is the pride
That cannot bear to be at fault
And merely human, fallible, a sinner
That holds us there
With cords we cannot break
Until we learn forgiveness
For ourselves.

It is not God
Demands this sacrifice
But man
For his appeasement
To whom God's love submits.

W.S. Beattie

139 A prayer

Dear Jesus, make me like what you were when you were six years old.

An Indian boy, 6 years

140 Two voices

Good Friday

Without listening,
Without knowing it,
The Lost man said:
'Give me a dead tree,
A green hill
With a hole in it;
A handful of nails,
Old rope;
A bag of spite,
Blanket of apathy,
A crate of cowardice;
Full spate of hate
And fear, a pinch
Of expediency –
And I will put out
The Light of Life
For ever.'

Easter Sunday

Fully persuaded,
The New man said:
'Give me one grain
Of faith;
One leap of hope;
One glance of love;
And each one
Pure, undiluted,
Genuine
As a diamond
Without flaw –
And I will banish
Death
And all his dominion
for ever.'

A.J. Lewis

141 Into freedom

Guardian of peace, shadowed on a cross to die.
Light feareth the cursed night.
A set picture of fear, engraved in the dark sky.
Bells ring his death . . .

But he shall rise, rise to the paradise,
Rise into freedom.

Helen Poore, 10 years

142 Prayer dance

Perfection
Was the child of thought
In a blue robe.
This was the wedding of movement and spirit
A reverence for her beloved.

She dances
As a stream flows clear,
Into an ecstasy of whirlpool.

Softly, arms caress light,
Light feet hold the marble pavement.

She sways, as by breeze,
To the soft inclination of the harp –

And yet she kneels heavily
As if the weight of wood and nails
Was thrown to her delicacy.

This is her way of praying:
A realisation
That His body was broken
While hers remained whole.

Catherine Payne, 16 years

143 Lament for Pilate

Born to witness
A hideous destruction
Sandals pacing and biting the paving
A man of lonely pity
Denied even Judas' strength
Tears of Mary stain his hands like wounds
Standing
Watching the Son sink behind the horizon
Light in the olive groves and gardens
Dimming and fading
Where night spreads like a disease
Greedily swallowing shadows
Intolerance and Rome
Bend and bare his neck, expecting punishment
And wind breathes the echo of his horror
Into skies
Pillars of a city lost
Filling his cold body with penitence
As a ritual accomplished
Denying his innocence.

Catherine Payne, 16 years

144 Suburban sins

The sin of Pilate,
  Cowardice and political time-serving.
The sin of Caiaphas,
  Spiritual pride and ecclesiastical time-serving.
The sins of the soldiers,
And of the crowd,
  Brutality.
  The lust for blood,
And blind following the majority.

These sins are not museum specimens, impaled on pins in
  glass cases, to be examined at leisure by those interested
  in religion.
Strange reactions of long ago people
In far away places.

No. Far from it. They are the sins
Of Acacia Avenue and Laburnum Grove;
Neat, semi-detached sins
Of respectable citizens
Living in respectable rows.
The sins of the milkman
And the neighbour who borrows your mower,
And the man who sits next to you on the eight-fifteen.
The sins of ordinary people,
Going daily to ordinary jobs,
And returning by six
To unspectacular homes and wives.
Your sins and my sins.
The sins of the children
Of our various parents.
The sins of the man in your shaving mirror.

It is these,
The penny-plain treacheries of John Citizen
and his unglamorous wife,
Which flame in the heat of the moment,
And flare to the sudden murder of God.

P.W. Turner

145 Day of waiting

It was their Sabbath
Days of quiet rest,
God's day, of all days,
That they spent bereft.
It was all ended now.
There was no action they could take,
Not even to annoint the body,
On such a holy day
Given for worship
And rememberance,
Day for the heart to break,
For He had died, but they
Were left alive, and comfortless
All that long Easter Sabbath
In Jerusalem.

W.S. Beattie

146 Resurrection to life

The churches loudly assert: we preach Christ crucified! But in doing so, they preach only half of the passion, and do only half their duty. The creed says: 'He was crucified, died, and was buried . . . the third day he rose again from the dead.' And again 'I believe in the resurrection of the body,' so that to preach Christ crucified is to preach half the truth.

It is the business of the Church to preach Christ born among men which is Christmas, Christ crucified which is Good Friday, and Christ risen which is Easter. And after Easter, till November and All Saints, and till Annunciation, the year belongs to the risen Lord: that is all the full flowering summer and the autumn of wheat and fruit. All belong to Christ risen.

But the churches insist on Christ crucified and rob us of the blossom and fruit of the year.

The *resurrection is to life*, not to death. Can I not then walk this earth in gladness being risen from sorrow? Is the flesh that was crucified become as poison to the crowds in the street, or is it a strong blossoming out of the earth's humus?

D.H. Lawrence

147 Resurrection morn

A sleepy mist beshrouds the town,
And in the shaded street,
Three stealthy figures move along,
Alert for a retreat.

Their arms are coiled round precious goods
Whose perfume fills the air,
Their voices echo, questioning,
And stammering with fear.

'We'll never move it, it's so big,
And we're not strong enough
It took four men to move the stone,
It's heavy, round and rough.'

At last they reached their promised goal,
Their faces reveal shock.
A gaping chasm lies in front,
'Someone's removed the rock!'

A piercing terror fills their hearts.
They know their Lord has gone,
But somehow they are calmed, until
They venture in the tomb.

The grave clothes lay there undisturbed,
But they feel reassured.
They realise with bubbling joy,
Death could not hold their Lord.

They rush straight out to tell the world,
His friends must quickly know.
'The Lord is risen, he is not dead,
He'll never leave us now.'

Maurita Horsler, 20 years

148 Once upon the crumbling roof

Once upon the crumbling roof
Of a windy church
A song-bird choked in the smoky air,
And all the world below
Died.

No one came to help him,
They thought there was nothing they could do.
So they did nothing.

Until at last a familiar stranger,
(Whom many thought they, perhaps, had seen before)
Arrived.
Alone he revived the creature
With just one warm whispering breath.

Many said, and believed,
There never had been any death
And flung away his truth and, smiling, sighed,
But the chattering song-bird was heard still singing,
Long after these doubters had, smiling, died.

John Jackson, 18 years

149 Street-wise

Christ is risen indeed, and goes before you into Galilee.

Your Galilee,
The Galilee of the modern industrial city,
Of the neon lights, and the multiple store,
Where you jostle Christ on the pavement
Among the plate-glass windows.

Galilee Street,
The street in which you live,
And where he waits to move in,
Fulfilling his promise to be with us,
Always,
Even to the end of the world.

Arise, shine,
Thy light is come,
And the glory of the Lord is risen upon thee.

P.W. Turner

150 Risen with him

If you believe that Christ has risen
   from the dead,
you must believe also that you yourselves
   have likewise risen with him . . .
and if you believe yourselves
   dead with Christ,
you must believe that
   you will also live with him;
and if you believe that Christ
   is dead to sin
and lives to God,
   you too must be dead to sin
and alive to God.

Origen

151 Resurrection now

When we begin to recognise the power of resurrection present
in the ordinary gritty routine of our daily lives, then we shall see
for ourselves that all that separates and injures and destroys is
being overcome by what unites and heals and creates. We shall
no longer have to ask where and when this happens, for we shall
have first-hand experience of it as we live as ordinary folk in the
ordinary world. But what, then, of resurrection as future, of
resurrection as our entry into the life of the world to come? If we
have been aware of resurrection in this life, then, and only then,
shall we be able or ready to receive the hope of final resurrection
after physical death. Resurrection as our final and ultimate future
can be known only by those who perceive resurrection with us
now encompassing all we are and do.

H.A. Williams, from _True Resurrection_

152 Resurrection all around

When the cold earth feels the sunshine;
Probing roots search deep for food,
Welcome Easter, welcome springtime,
Jesus lives and God is good.

When the crocus braves the weather;
Lifts its head to greet the sky,
Welcome Easter, welcome springtime,
Jesus lives and God is nigh.

When a friendship, sadly broken,
Starts again its warmth to find,
Welcome Easter, welcome springtime,
Jesus lives and God is kind.

When a family, spoilt by quarrels,
Cools its temper, hurt removes,
Welcome Easter, welcome springtime,
Jesus lives and God is love.

When the poor, the homeless, hungry,
Reach for help, no longer sad,
Welcome Easter, welcome springtime,
Jesus lives and God is glad.

When the Church sings Easter gladness,
Voices raised, a faith to share,
Welcome Easter, welcome springtime,
Jesus lives and God is there.

Donald Hilton

153 The day of Pentecost

The path of destruction
Is all one can see
Of the riotous wind.
It rips houses
From their foundations
And plucks trees
From the ground.
It makes families homeless.
This is
Devastation.
Then there is the gentle breeze
Cooling the hot brow
In summer.
Gently rustling the green leaves.
But no wind was
So gentle
And yet
So mighty
As the coming of the Holy Spirit.

Jenny Mabbott, 14 years

154 Wind and fire

The fire of the Spirit was not a general flame,
not bushfire, contagious, engulfing all.
But a flame on each one.
So we never claim to carry the flame
from place to place,
as though the Spirit is our private box of matches
or little incense pot.

But the fire is there, already, now.
It shines in the eyes of the eager,
joyful, trusting children of God.
It is there in the hands of the healers
and servers and bearers of heavy loads.
It is local. A flame on each one.

There is also the wind, and the wind travels;
across oceans and mountains, always in movement.
May God let us be the breezes of the Spirit,
which fan the flames and fill the house
and let the smoking flax burst into a glory of fire.
    Wind and fire, life of the Spirit,
    universal and local, be our energy;
    wind and fire, elements of Pentecost,
    power for the Kingdom, be power for our city.

Bernard Thorogood

155 Like a strong wind

Dear God,
I am thinking about the wind,
And about You.

I can't see the wind,
But it's very real.
I can feel the wind.
And I can see what the wind does,
Ruffling my hair,
Moving the leaves on the trees,
Blowing into the sails to carry a boat along.

Dear God,
I don't understand all about You,
But I know You are real.
I know You can touch my inside thoughts,
I know You are always there.
I can't see You,
But You are real. And You love me.

You understand all about me;
I can talk to You,
And listen to You inside my thoughts.
I'm like a small boat with a sail,
And You can move me along
To try things with You and for You,
To adventure with You and for You.

Thank You, God,
For being God.   *Amen.*

Lilian Cox

156 Dream Church

This is the Church of my dreams –
The Church of the warm heart,
Of the open mind,
Of the adventurous spirit;
The Church that cares,
That heals hurt lives,
That comforts old people,
That challenges youth;
That knows no divisions of culture or class;
No frontiers, geographical or social,
The Church that enquires as well as affirms,
That looks forward as well as backward;
The Church of the Master,
The Church of the people;
High as the ideals of Jesus,
Low as the humblest human;
A working Church,
A worshipping Church,
A winsome Church;
A Church that interprets truth in terms of truth;
That inspires courage for this life and hope for the life to come;
A Church of courage;
A Church of all good men –
The Church of the living God.

Anon

157 Circle of dance

God, you invite us to dance in delight,
shaping and forming in figures of grace.
We move to the pulse of creation's music
and rejoice to be part of the making of earth.

**Praise in the making, the sharing, the moving;
praise to the God who dances with us.**

In the steps of Jesus we reach to our partners,
touching and holding and finding our strengths.
Together we move into patterns of freedom,
and rejoice to be part of the sharing of hope.

**Praise in the making, the sharing, the moving;
praise to the God who dances with us.**

We whirl and spin in the Spirit's rhythm,
embracing the world with our circles of joy.
Together we dance for salvation and justice,
and rejoice to be part of the moving of love.

**Praise in the making, the sharing, the moving;
praise to the God who dances with us.**

Amen

Jan Berry

BELONGING

How good and pleasant it is
to live together as brothers in unity!
It is as if the dew of Hermon were falling
on the mountains of Zion.
There the Lord bestows his blessing,
life for evermore.

Psalm 133.1,3

One and all they kept up their daily attendance at the temple, and breaking bread in their homes, they shared their meals with unaffected joy, as they praised God and enjoyed the favour of the whole people. And day by day the Lord added new converts to their number.

Acts 2.46–47

By authority of the grace God has given me I say to everyone among you: do not think too highly of yourself, but form a sober estimate based on the message of faith that God has dealt to each of you. For just as in a single human body there are many limbs and organs, all with different functions, so we who are united with Christ, though many, form one body, and belong to one another as its limbs and organs.

Romans 12.3–5

Love is patient and kind. Love envies no one, is never boastful, never conceited, never rude; love is never selfish, never quick to take offence. Love keeps no score of wrongs, takes no pleasure in the sins of others, but delights in the truth. There is nothing love cannot face; there is no limit to its faith, its hope, its endurance.

1 Corinthians 13.4–5

For he is himself our peace. Gentiles and Jews, he has made the two one, and in his own body of flesh and blood has broken down the barrier of enmity which separated them, for he annulled the law with its rules and regulations, so as to create out of the two a single new humanity in himself, thereby making peace. This was his purpose, to reconcile the two in a single body to God through the cross, by which he killed the enmity.

Ephesians 2.14–16

158 One and many

. . . each person is unique, and created to the image and likeness of God. Each then reflects God's beauty, intelligence, power, freedom and love. We are all called to be free, autonomous, self-determining, masters of our own decisions. At the same time we are social beings, and personal self-determination can be fully achieved only in harmony with the social self-determination of groups to which we belong.

Catholic Bishop of Australia

159 Contact

Reach out my hand to touch
My neighbour, friend,
Or kith and kin.

Not quite;
Not far enough;
The gap's too great.
So I must lean,
Further and further,
Hand stretching out to hand.

What if I fall;
Lose balance and
         Upset
My equilibrium?

Perhaps I shall have to change my ground.

Donald Hilton

160 Nothing more than love

Love is a great thing,
Yea, a great and thorough good;
For it carries a burden that is no burden,
And makes everything that is bitter, sweet and savoury.
Nothing is sweeter than love,
Nothing more courageous,
Nothing fuller or better in heaven and earth;
Because love is born of God.
He that loveth, flieth, runneth and rejoiceth,
He is free, and cannot be held in.

Love feels no burden, thinks nothing of trouble,
Attempts what is above its strength,
Thinks nothing impossible.
Though weary, love is not tired;
Though alarmed, it is not confounded:
but as a lively flame and burning torch,
It forces its way upwards,
And securely passes through all.

Thomas à Kempis

161 When wrong is right

I quarrelled with my brother,
I don't know what about,
One thing led to another
And somehow we fell out.
The start of it was slight,
The end of it was strong,
He said he was right,
I knew he was wrong!
We hated one another.
The afternoon turned black.
Then suddenly my brother
Thumped me on the back,
And said, 'Oh come along!
We can't go on all night –
I was in the wrong.'
So he was in the right.

Eleanor Farjeon

162 O octopus

Love is like an octopus
It looks so soft and squishy.
How graceful are its tentacles
And eyes divinely dishy.
O octopus, I yearn for you
Since I am octopoidal too
You shall be mine,
Let us entwine.
Our tentacles shall never part
Till one of us, right to the heart
Is eaten up. Which shall that be?
I'll make quite sure it isn't me!

W.S. Beattie

163 It's mine

I made a parcel of my woes
Packaged with all my skill
And hawked it round the town.
But no one wanted it.
Surprise, surprise.
The question is
If someone had
Could I have borne to let it go.
It's mine, you see,
Uniquely mine
To make the most of.
What would I be without it?

W.S. Beattie

164 Sorry

Things went wrong today, God:
You know they did,
I know they did.
Show me where it was my fault;
I'll think about that, now,
And I won't dodge or make excuses . . .

Yes God, I do see where I was wrong.
I'm sorry, dear God,
Truly sorry,
It was my fault –
Please forgive me.
Is there anything I ought to do
To put things right?
I'll think about that now, with You . . .

Yes, I see what I ought to do;
Help me, God, to do it straight away.
You will help me, I know.

And then You'll give me a new start.
Thank You, God,
Thank You for my new start.   *Amen.*

Lilian Cox

165 Dumb words

I looked –
  And wondered if those
    Penetrating eyes,
      Smiling, appreciating and answering
      Every spoken question in the
        Crowded, smoke filled room
          Could intercept and decipher
            The unspoken yet urgent question
            My eyes were asking you?

Ann Hunter

166 On the bridge

I asked
If you were lonely.

I like to be alone
You said.

Yet we stood
On the bridge
Talking
Till the morning.

I. Choonara

167 Conversation in November

You spoke of partings:
I, of foxes' trails through snow
and ashen birds
winging thread-drawn on
November skies.

You spoke of solitude:
and I of rattling grass
frost dried on the crackling path
and white-rimmed leaves
curled on brittle stems.

You spoke of sorrows:
I, of hands pushed deeper
into throbbing warmths of pockets
fingers cold with speaking
gestures on to chilly air.

You spoke of dying;
then I was silent –
torn between growing shadows
and the snowflakes
melting in your hair.

Jan Walker, 17 years

168 In closing

In closing
might I ask
If we meet
sometime next year
Shall we smile
as friend
Or shall we stumble
over memories
and be confused?

Jane Elliot

169 All alone

Alone, alone
In a wall of stone,
All the love in this world has gone.
Now I'm in this wall of stone.

Cut off from people in the world
All alone, all alone in this wall of stone,
I hear the rushing of the sea.
I wish I was not me.

David Salter, 9 years

170 Lost friends

Never forgotten,
Always there.
An echo of
A memory
Spins round and round.

Christopher Garry, 9 years

171 Lost friends

No happiness, no joy,
No feelings, no fear,
But tears of sadness.

Joy is dead,
Sadness creeps,
Tears flow,
Terrifying cries,
Death dawns;
My friend is lost.
Craters of nothingness,
Happiness, joy, all is gone.

Amanda Bird, 10 years

172 The future present

A wise rabbi was walking along a road when he saw a man planting a tree. The rabbi asked him, "How many years will it take for this tree to bear fruit?" The man answered that it would take seventy years. The rabbi asked, "Are you so fit and strong that you expect to live that long and eat its fruit?" The man answered, "I found a fruitful world because my forefathers planted for me. So I will do the same for my children."

The Jewish Midrash

173 Prayer for the city

Pressing in upon each other
in the city are –
wealth and poverty,
glamour and squalor,
bright lights and dark alleys,
hygienic wonders of glass,
steel and concrete
and crumbling
rat-infested slums.

There is tension in the city,
in the board-room, in the typing pool.
There is haste in the city,
in the office, in the street.
Shoulders jostle,
but rarely is there meeting.
People throng in the city,
but loneliness is in their midst.

Pray for the needs concealed
behind the city's
mask of well-being.
Pray for:
– The old-old young,
   with adventure already turned sour.
– The desperate seekers after accommodation.
– The pavement dwellers and the drop-outs.
– The human jackals preying upon their fellows.
– The decent, honest people, forever hurrying
   yet seldom asking where they are going.

Edmund Banyard

174 Interconnection

This above all is precious and remarkable
How we put ourselves in one another's care,
How in spite of everything, we trust each other.

Fishermen at whatever point they are dipping and lifting
On the dark green swell they partly think of as home
Hear the gale warnings that fly to them like gulls.

The scientists study the weather for love of studying it,
And not specially for love of the fishermen,
And the wireless engineers do the transmission for love
    of wireless,

But how it adds up is that when the terrible white malice
Of the waves high as cliffs is let loose to seek a victim
The fishermen are somewhere else and so not drowned.

John Wain

175 The old priest

The whitewashed walls are peeling,
And the stone is showing through,
There are cobwebs on the ceiling,
And bats in the belfry too.

The old brown pews are beyond repair,
The hymn books are worn and old,
The old black priest with whiting hair
Is shivering in the cold.

He carries out his service
As though the folk were there,
But the whitewashed walls are peeling
And in each book, a tear.

He's old and very weary
And he can hardly see
But he says the time's gone quickly
For everyone but he.

Bridget Rawlence, 11 years

176 Memory

The vicar slowly climbs the pulpit stair.
His wife sits fumbling in the organ loft.
No congregation, 'What's the point?' they say.
Even the grave-digger has gone away.

As he begins his solitary sermon
He stops, remembering some other days.
He was a student, full of new ideas.
Here was his mission. He would save the world.

Now who is saved? He cannot even tell.
The newspaper is always three days late.
It was not he who saved them. That he knows.
Rotting away, with ivied monuments.

There sits his wife, wrapped in a tartan rug.
Playing 'Jerusalem' to please the mice.
'What life is this?' he thinks. But numbed by the years
His brain does not reply, just sleeps again.

Clarissa Browne, 14 years

177 Together for others

Through constant caring for the well-being of a particular church and of those fellowships of churches and those Church enterprises to which it is committed, Christians learn together how to make a common Christian judgement expressing practical love and obedience to God. They grow in discipleship when together they seek the Holy Spirit's guidance and each tests his own attitude in the light of attitudes adopted by others. Members meet, in the domestic life of the Church, bringing experience gained in the daily life of the world which helps to suggest where the paths of wisdom and of service should run. From their meeting they go out again to daily life with fresh experience of reaching Christian decisions in the fellowship of the Church, strengthened to share again with men of all faiths and of none in making decisions which will best uphold the dignity and well-being of all who are affected. In this process God is able to make Church membership fruitful beyond the Church's domestic life. He teaches his Church again and again that it does not live for itself but for its ministry of love and service and witness, in the local neighbourhood of each particular church and to the ends of the earth.

The Congregational Church of England and Wales,
from *A Declaration of Faith*

178   Friends' meeting

very nearly a non-swimmer
I have just enough breaststroke
to save my soul.

Sundays, I take deep breaths
and go in to test my strength.

debris of house and home
bump and bruise
my outstretched hands;

tangles of the week and work
loop round my legs
to lure me down;

but often, amazed,
I achieve my width;
buoyed up, it seems,
by the quiet strokes
of others, friends,
mutually striving
to stay afloat,

and aiming in the
same direction.

Nadine Vokins

179 The first day

Sunday's the day for holy work,
For each to do his bit
To keep the church afloat.
To sing, give lifts,
Or count the offering
And deal with business
In between the praise.
To get the latest news,
To see who's there
And note the absentees
With speculation.

Here, week by week we gather,
Mingle the edges of our lives
And interchange a stream of words,
appropriate sentiments,
The social lubricant.
Yet of that Word we seldom speak
One to another
In ordinary human talk,
As if he were a precious ikon set apart,
His life a puzzle that defeats us,
His gospel news gone stale.

Is it a charitable silence that we keep?
Or are our tongues held back by modesty?
Or are we naked and in rags
But too polite to mention it?

A loyal activism,
A stoic silence,
A life kept private,
These we choose.
This pattern we can cope with.
Only, just now and then, a word
Of someone who has searched and found
Or has been found,
A word of joy not quite impossible
Cracks open our defence
And thaws the heart
In brief emotion –
Inconvenient, not quite proper,
Especially in church,
But real and human
And perhaps divine?

W.S. Beattie

180 All shall be saved

All, all shall be saved!
God's love desires that none
He loves, shall be destroyed
For all are loved by Him
And loved to the uttermost.

God's love is cross shaped
Each hard wooden spar
Symbolising the link between
The Heaven of God's saving grace
That reaches down to mortal man
And stretches out through
The arms of Christ
Touching mankind in all
Its glory and decay. Love
Is the saving power and link
Which holds us all
In the motherly embrace
And by that love
All are gathered in.

Gerald Gardiner

181 The vine

All my fruit is yours for you are mine.
The root and stem from which my tendrils twine;
You are the warmth that swells my tender grapes.

My leaves are hands uplifted to your light;
Each palm grows bright to catch the falling sun.
And when the waiting nets of night
Are wide to hold earth's ripeness we are one –
Root, branch, and leaf and rounding fruit begun
In life's full circle.
White root, go deep
That in your tunnelled darkness I may sleep;
Strong branch, reach high
Till my green hands, glad servers of the sun,
Receive the cup of water and of fire
And find it brimmed with wine –
I drink you drain you till my life in yours
Is yours in mine.

Phoebe Hesketh

182 Christian Aid Week

God guide me with your wisdom
God chastise me with your justice
God help me with your mercy
God protect me with your strength
that together we may seek peace
that together we may find justice
that together we may be merciful
that together we may have wisdom
   to reach out to the poor and needy
   to shelter the refugee
   to campaign for the homeless
   to work for the integrity of creation
God fill us with your fullness
God shield us with your shade
God fill us with your grace
that for the sake of your anointed Son
we may be His hands and feet
in the world.

Kate McIlhagga

183 Nondescript

He stood before the court in nondescript clothes,
no papers, no fixed address.
The judge cleared his throat,
'Have you anything to say
before I pass sentence?'
What might have been his answer
had the prisoner the gift of speech
and the court the gift of hearing?

'I am condemned because your law
allows no place for me.
My crimes I freely admit:-
I am homeless, seeking shelter
where I may rear my family in modest decency.
I am stateless, seeking country
where I may belong by right in God's good earth.
I am destitute, claiming a share of the wealth
that is our common heritage.
I am a sinner, needing aid from fellow sinners.'

'You will dispose of me according to your law,
but you will not so easily dispose of him
who owns me citizen in his kingdom.
He frowns on crimes your law condones;
pride, selfishness and greed,
self-righteousness,
the worship of all things material
and the refusal to acknowledge me as brother.'

'By your law I stand condemned;
but one day you must answer
to the master of us all
for the havoc caused by your law
in his realm.'

Edmund Baynard

184 Famine

Large, blank, lack-lustre eyes
Stare uncomprehendingly
At the scorched and bleached landscape.
A land without rain.
A land without food.
Its only harvest, millions of people.
People without bread or hope;
Matchstick limbs and skin
That flaps like sacking over a framework
Once recognisably a human form.
Can this be a man
Made in God's own image?

Hear a mother's keening cry
As she holds to her dry breast
The lifeless shell of her only child,
Born to die;
And the mother's hope dies too.

Can this bleak existence be
What we call human life?
Does there have to be
Such hell on earth
Before our Christian souls are stirred?
Does God suffer and die
With his hungry, helpless people,
Preferring their hell
To our heaven of affluence?
Will our wealth and our mountains of grain
Represent our judgement
Before the throne of God?

'O brother man
Fold to thy heart thy brother.'
Feel his bones and sores;
Feel his hunger and despair.
Look into his eyes if you dare.
He wants not your guilt
But your compassion.
He wants not your sorrow
But the conversion of your will
That says, 'My brother, my sister,
The world is ours.
Let us share its wealth together.
Your hunger is my hunger;
My wealth is your wealth.'

Gerald Gardiner

185 **A parable**

Once upon a time there was a class
and the students expressed disapproval of their teacher.
Why should they be concerned with
global interdependency, global problems
and what others of the world were thinking, feeling and
doing?
And the teacher said she had a dream in which she
saw one of her students fifty years from today.
The student was angry and said,
'Why did I learn so much detail about the past
and the administration of my country
and so little about the world?'
He was angry because no one told him
that as an adult he would be faced
almost daily with problems of a
global interdependent nature, be they
problems of peace, security, quality
of life, food, inflation, or scarcity
of natural resources.
The angry student found he was the
victim as well as the beneficiary.
'Why was I not warned? Why was
I not better educated? Why
did my teachers not tell me about
the problems and help me understand
I was a member of an interdependent human race?'
With even greater anger the student shouted,
'You helped me extend my hands with incredible machines,
my eyes with telescopes and microscopes,
my ears with telephones, radios, and sonar,
my brain with computers,
but you did not help me extend
my heart, love, concern
to the entire human family.
You, teacher, gave me half a loaf.'

Jon Rye Kinghorn

CALLED

While tending the sheep of his father-in-law Jethro, priest of Midian, Moses led the flock along the west side of the wilderness and came to Horeb, the mountain of God. There an angel of the Lord appeared to him as a fire blazing out from a bush. Although the bush was on fire, it was not being burned up, and Moses said to himself, 'I must go across and see this remarkable sight. Why ever does the bush not burn away?' When the Lord saw that Moses had turned aside to look, he called to him out of the bush, 'Moses, Moses!' He answered, 'Here I am!' God said, 'Do not come near! Take off your sandals, for the place where you are standing is holy ground.' Then he said, 'I am the God of your father, the God of Abraham, Isaac, and Jacob.' Moses hid his face, for he was afraid to look at God.

Exodus 3.1–6

One of the seraphim flew to me, carrying in his hand a glowing coal which he had taken from the altar with a pair of tongs. He touched my mouth with it and said,

'This has touched your lips;
now your iniquity is removed
and your sin wiped out.'

I heard the Lord saying, 'Whom shall I send? Who will go for us?' I said: 'Here I am! Send me'. He replied: 'Go, tell this people:

However hard you listen, you will never understand.
However hard you look, you will never perceive.'

Isaiah 6.6–9

After washing their feet he put on his garment and sat down again. 'Do you understand what I have done for you?' he asked. 'You call me Teacher and Lord, and rightly so, for that is what I am. Then if I, your Lord and Teacher have washed your feet, you ought to wash one another's feet. I have set you an example: you are to do as I have done for you. In very truth I tell you, a servant is not greater than his master, nor a messenger than the one who sent him. If you know this, happy are you if you act upon it.'

John 13.12–17

186 Meditation

Make time to sit in comfort
to breathe deeply
to relax in the presence of God
like a cat asleep on a chair
or a rabbit sunnily on a path:

   The loving one, who made you
   who yearned over you in the womb
   who cherished you as a baby
   who tendered you as a child
   who gave you glimpses of glory
   from your pram
   who moulded you
   inciting cries for justice
   the one whose loving arm is always
   under your head
   says
   have no fear for I have redeemed you
   I call you by name
   And you are mine.

   I . . . am loved by God.
     Keep silence in that thought.

Kate McIlhagga

187 Still, like a child

Like a child
still in the womb
I pray, my knees bent
and my head bowed.

Like a child
still in the womb
I wait, trembling at the largeness
of the world
into whose incomprehensible hands

You will deliver me.

Andrew M. Rudd

188 A Meditation

God has created me to do him some definite service. He has committed some work to me which he has not committed to another. I have my mission. I may never know it in this world, but I shall be told it in the next.

I am a link in the chain, a bond of connection between persons. He has not created me for naught.

I shall do good. I shall do his work. I shall be an angel of peace, a preacher of truth in my own place, while not intending it, if I do but keep his commandments.

Therefore will I trust him. Wherever, whatever I am, I can never be thrown away. If I am in sickness, my sicknness may serve him; in perplexity, my perplexity may serve him; if I am in sorrow, my sorrow may serve him.

He does nothing in vain. He knows what he is about. He may take away my friends, he may throw me among strangers. He may make me feel desolate, make my spirits sink, hide my future from me . . . still . . . he knows what he is about.

John Henry Newman

189 Shall I betray him?

Shall I tell the Romans?
Or shall I not?
If I do
There will be money – quite a lot.

I'll give it to the poor
Like Jesus said I should
He'll be pleased no doubt.
Yes! I think I could.

Let him prove he's the Son of God
By saving himself from the cross
Then they won't bother him
And they'll see who's boss.

Yes! I will tell the Romans
There's no doubt about that
After the Passover supper
So Jesus won't smell a rat.

Samantha Milton, 11 years
Rebecca Morely, 11 years

190 Calling women

No woman without an overwhelming sense of a call from outside herself would willingly embrace the isolation and pain that comes with confessing she believes she is called to priesthood. Many women tell of trying to shut out such a call, to turn their backs on it, as Jeremiah tried to turn his back on his call to be a prophet. Many, like him, find they can do no other than be faithful to their call whatever that brings. To deny the call would be to deny the voice of God; to respond to the call is to be divided sometimes from colleagues and close friends and to be rejected by the Church.

Mary Tanner, from *Feminine in the Church*

191

Women who claim a call to priesthood are dismissed as misguided, deluded, arrogant, status-seeking. How can women receive a call to priesthood when the Church does not provide for the testing of such a call? It is implied that no call can be received as long as the institutional Church makes no provision for testing it.

But surely to dismiss the testimony from a growing number of women to be called by God to a priestly ministry is to do less than justice to the Church tradition itself. The God whom Christians claim to have faith in is a creator God who does not remain remote from that which he has created but moves always towards his creations in love. He is a God who from the earliest time, from the patriarch Abraham, takes the initiative and calls men and women into relation with himself. He calls them to serve him and to serve one another in him. Indeed, every Christian baptized into the death of Christ rises through the waters of baptism and is called to a life of service. We acknowledge and say 'yes' to that call in confirmation, and reaffirm our response at every Eucharist. Christian discipleship is one of responding to a call from God. To be a Christian is to know that it belongs to the nature of God that he calls us out of the world to serve him.

Mary Tanner, from *Feminine in the Church*

192   Careful calculations

You asked for my hands
that you might use them for your purpose.
I gave them for a moment then withdrew them
for the work was hard.

You asked for my mouth
to speak out against injustice.
I gave you a whisper that I might not be accused.

You asked for eyes
to see the pain of poverty.
I closed them for I did not want to see.

You asked for my life
that you might work through me.
I gave a small part that I might not get too involved.

Lord, forgive my calculated efforts to serve you,
only when it is convenient for me to do so,
only in those places where it is safe to do so,
and only with those who make it easy to do so.

Father, forgive me,
renew me
send me out
as a usable instrument
that I might take seriously
the meaning of your cross.

Joe Seremane

193 On crosses

Take up your cross, the preacher said.
No need.
It's dumped upon my back.
I have to carry it as best I can,
And while I can.
Remember
Jesus fell
Beneath the cross.

Crosses come all shapes and sizes,
One for me, one for you,
One for each mortal born to die.
But not the one that takes our fancy,
The one that we would carry gracefully
And rest upon with elegance.
Ours is the one that fits us,
The shadow of our own particular good.
That cross is inescapable,
Intimately known,
Part of myself.
It gives form and shape to my being
As the skeleton,
The symbol of my death
Structures my living body.

Do I bear it? Does it bear me?
I shift without rest in the rhythms of life
My flesh torn by the nails
My life-blood spilling on the ground.
This cross, so hard and so intractable,
Is this what I am to become?

Afterwards they took the body down.
What happened to it then we are still arguing.
But the symbol that spans the world
Is the living cross
To which He was annealed.

W.S. Beattie

194 Touched

The rough bark
pressed against
my forehead
as I clung
to the tree
and let
grief's healing tears
flow.

    The strong support
    of his forearms
    under mine
    as He said:
    'Don't cling
    but go and tell
    the others'.

The wet grass
under my feet
as I flew . . .

    The warm touch
    of their hands
    as we shared
    the good news;
    the light of Christ
    shining
    from our eyes,
    to the glory of God.

Kate McIlhagga
(John 20.11–18)

195 The Spirit

You can shatter all my dreams and all I've worked for,
You can tear me at the seams and slam shut each door,
You can hit me all you like,
Then watch me fall and fail to fight,
But you cannot take the Spirit from within me.

You can laugh until I cry, and then forget me,
You can build my hopes up high, and then reject me,
You can tell me there's no hope,
And then watch me fail to cope,
But you cannot take the Spirit from within me.

You can tell me it's not true – the way I'm feeling,
You can find me something new that's more 'appealing',
But the call is here inside,
I am here, I will not hide,
And you will not take the Spirit from within me,
NO! You will not crush the Spirit from within.

Anne Sardeson

196 The penetrating word

The Word of God is alive and active.

We do not open the Scriptures to have our prejudices confirmed but to have them shattered. Whilst the essential nature of God does not change, God's Word is spoken at particular times and to particular situations. When the Israelites set about the conquest of Canaan the Word, as they heard it, required them to destroy all in their path. The only alternative they knew was plunder, the taking of slaves and, inevitably, the adoption of local baals. So that Word to them, grim as it sounds to us, was a call to wholeheartedness and total commitment. Most surely God still requires wholeheartedness and commitment but the mode in which it will be expressed for us will be different. It might be a call to dispose of idols: money, power, the trappings of success. Instead of destroying enemies we may be called to build bridges that could change enemies to friends. These are merely illustrations. I cannot know what God will have for you any more than I can know God's next Word for me before it is spoken. What we can expect is that it will be a contemporary Word. It will contain all the fullness of Christ and – since we find consistently throughout the Scriptures that those who hear the Word were shaken by it – it is unlikely to be comfortable.

Edmund Banyard

197   A holy rage

"What is therefore the task of the preacher today? Shall I answer: faith, hope and love? That sounds beautiful. But I would rather say: courage. No, even that is not challenging enough to be the *whole* truth . . . Our task today is recklessness . . . For what we (as church) lack is most assuredly not psychology or literature. We lack a holy rage . . ."

A holy rage. The recklessness which comes from the knowledge of God and humanity. The ability to rage when justice lies prostrate on the streets and when the lie rages across the face of the earth. A holy anger about things that are wrong in the world. To rage against the ravaging of God's earth and the destruction of God's world. To rage when little children must die of hunger while the tables of the rich are sagging with food. To rage at the senseless killing of so many and against the madness of militarism. To rage at the lie that calls the threat of death and the strategy of destruction "peace". To rage against the complacency of so many in the church who fail to see that we shall live only by the truth, and that our fear will be the death of us all . . . To restlessly seek that recklessness that will challenge, and to seek to change human history until it conforms to the norms of the kingdom of God.

Alan Boesak, from *Walking on Thorns*

198 Unexpected gifts

I asked God for strength that I might achieve;
I was made weak that I might learn humbly to obey.

I asked for help that I might do greater things;
I was given infirmity that I might do better things.

I asked for riches that I might be happy;
I was given poverty that I might be wise.

I asked for power that I might have the praise of others;
I was given weakness that I might feel the need of God.

I asked for all things that I might enjoy life;
I was given life that I might enjoy all things.

I got nothing that I asked for – but everything I'd hoped for.
My unspoken prayers were answered. I am among all men
   most richly blessed!

An unknown soldier of the 19th century

199 In their own experience

He comes to us as one unknown, without a name, as of old, by
the lake-side, he came to those men who knew him not. He speaks
to us the same word: 'Follow thou me!' and sets us to the task
which he has to fulfil for our time. He commands. And to those
who obey him, whether they be wise or simple, he will reveal
himself in the toils, the conflicts, the sufferings which they shall
pass through in his fellowship, and as an ineffable mystery, they
shall learn in their own experience who he is.

Albert Schweitzer, from *The Quest for the Historical Jesus*

200 No sacrifice

It is true that missionaries have difficulties to encounter; but what
great enterprise was ever accomplished without difficulty? For my
part I have never ceased to rejoice that God has appointed me
to such an office. People talk of the sacrifice I have made in
spending so much of my time in Africa. Can that be called a
sacrifice which simply paid back a small part of a great debt? It
is emphatically no sacrifice. I know that in a few years I shall be
cut off in that country. Do you carry on the work which I have
begun. I leave it with you!

David Livingstone

201 The foot washing

Choral harmonies spiral on the incensed air
Lifted on the organ's resonant tones
And drift with prayer thoughts
Above the six tall, flickering, altar candles
And the wall painted host of heavenly places.
'Holy, holy, holy is the Lord God of hosts.
Heaven and earth are full of His glory.'

Bring now water, towel and basin.
Man of God, now become servant,
Kneel before your congregation.
Roll your sleeves! Give menial service.
Take these feet, young, old, misshapen,
That have walked and worked for God.
See their feet today, not faces,
Handle them with loving care
and wash them. Pouring on the water,
Wiping them with gentleness.
As the servant kiss those feet
As a slave might greet his master.
This is the sacrament of service.
This was the action of the Master, and He
Has given us this great example.
Man from God. Now become servant.

Gerald Gardiner

202 Servant and master always

Climbing the stairs
to that
Upper Room,
each was shut in his
separate,
private world
of dreams and nightmares.
They sat at table
in uncomfortable neighbourliness,
the dust of the streets still on them;
together,
yet not together;
each man imprisoned within himself.

Water and basin stood untouched,
none willing to be servant
to the others
until Jesus,
rising,
took towel,
water and basin
and washed their feet,
servant and master in one.

Even as they protested
they knew that it had always been so;
always would be so.
his body broken for them;
his life poured out
that they might live;
and with them
every soul
in every land
in every age.

Faces change;
yet still to that Table
come disciples
soiled by the world,
divided . . .

Again the Lord comes as servant
and we know,
amid all that poisons
human relationships,
we are a part
of that broken body,
renewed by that freely given life.

Beyond all words
and symbols,
HIMSELF,
the Life,
the Truth,
the Way.

Edmund Banyard

203 Snow

Hold out your arms, trees
feel the silence of the snow –
its contemplation.

we too, wait
on the verge
of awakening.

Cecily Taylor

204 At one with nature

We sat by the roadside and scooped the dust with our hands and made little piles in the gutters. Then we slid through the grass and lay on our backs and just stared at the empty sky. There was nothing to do. Nothing moved or happened, nothing happened at all except summer. Small heated winds blew over our faces, dandelion seeds floated by, burnt sap and roast nettles tingled our nostrils togther with the dull rust smell of dry ground. The grass was June high and had come up with a rush, a massed entanglement of species, crested with flowers and spears of wild wheat, and coiled with clambering vetches, the whole of it humming with blundering bees and flickering with scarlet butterflies. Chewing grass on our backs, the grass scaffolding the sky, the summer was all we heard; cuckoos crossed distances on chains of cries, flies buzzed and choked in the ears, and the saw-toothed chatter of mowing-machines drifted on waves of air from the fields.

Laurie Lee, from *Cider with Rosie*

205 Under authority

For, as far back as I can remember anything, I was somehow aware that my parents lived under the same kind of authority as that which, through them, was communicated to me. I could see that my parents too behaved as though they, *even they*, were not their own; and had they behaved as though they were their own and might do what they liked and might ask of me merely what they liked to ask, their authority over me could not have had the character which I actually felt it to possess.

John Baillie, from *Our Knowledge of God*

206 God reigns

When we deliberate, God reigns;
When we decide wisely, he reigns;
When we decide foolishly, he reigns;
When we serve him in humble loyalty, he reigns;
When we serve him self-assertively; he reigns;
When we rebel and seek to withhold our service,
He reigns: The Alpha and the Omega,
Which was, and which is, and which is to come,
The Almighty.

William Temple

207 The Martha Church

Here is a pair of hands.
And here
Within the Martha church
Are things to do, time-honoured, recognised.
And these are good,
They bind us to a fellowship of service,
Give us stability, a place, a limit,
A defence against the vastness
That else might overwhelm.
Take on this discipline,
Accept its irksomeness,
Or else who knows
What labour of Prometheus
Might swallow you.
Or else you might be lost
Living within a formless void
Perplexed to choose and purposeless.
Rest yourself here
In useful labour.
Occupy the time.
But do not doubt
That in the end all limits fail.
Be glad to know
That even here the wind may blow.

W.S. Beattie

208 Worship

Worship is the submission of all our nature to God.
It is the quickening of conscience by his holiness;
the nourishment of mind with his truth;
the purifying of the imagination by his beauty;
the opening of the heart to his love;
and the surrender of will to his purpose.

William Temple

209 Lines of dependence

There are all kinds of men
Who have done me good turns,
That I still never think about,
Not for a minute;
Yet if I were making up
That sort of grace,
They would all of them have
To be in it.

One man made up stories,
Another wrote verses
I found, and I liked,
And I read till I knew them.
Another one saw
All the things they had written,
Then, being an artist,
He drew them.

Another took wood
And a saw and some glue,
And put each of them just
In the place that would need it;
So that is the chair
Where I sit with my book
And am so much at ease
As I read it.

I'm forgetting the one
Who read tale after tale
When I was too young
To know letter from letter,
And the other who taught me them,
Till in the end
I could read for myself –
Which was better.

Rodney Bennett

210 The collar

Why mark the person with a badge
which holds his neck in stiff embrace?
Why dress him up and mark him down
as stranger to the human race?

To pedestal him guru-like
and say he's far above the crowd
is cheating, making him pretend
he's different, holy on a cloud.

But badges carry conduct rules
from skinhead shout to schoolgirl glance
and I know well the collar speaks
a way of life that's not just chance.

It makes me steady, quiet, plain,
It silences my sudden wrath,
It keeps my eyes upon the way
not drawn to flames like flippant moth.

There are some days when your control
around the neck this dog can lead;
but rather would I know the ties
by which a cleric's heart is freed.

Bernard Thorogood

211 It is the Lord!

Methought that in a solemn church I stood.
Its marble acres, worn with knees and feet,
Lay spread from door to door, from street to street.
Midway the form hung high upon the rood
Of him who gave his life to be our good;
Beyond, priests flitted, bowed and murmured meet,
Among the candles shining still and sweet.
Men came and went, and worshipped as they could –
And still their dust a woman with her broom,
Bowed to her work, keep sweeping to the door.
Then I saw, slow through all the pillared gloom,
Across the church a silent figure come;
'Daughter,' it said, 'thou sweepest well my floor!'
'It is the Lord!' I cried, and saw no more.

George Macdonald

212 Sunday

My mother's strongest religious feeling
Was that Catholics were a sinister lot;
She would hardly trust even a lapsed one.
My father was a lapsed Catholic.

Yet we were sent to Sunday school.
Perhaps in the spirit that others
Were sent to public schools. It
Might come in useful later on.

In Sunday school a sickly adult
Taught the teachings of a sickly lamb
To a gathering of sickly children.

It was a far cry from that brisk person
Who created the heaven and the earth in
Six days and then took Sunday off.

The churches were run by a picked crew
Of bad actors radiating insincerity.
Not that one thought of them in that way,
One merely disliked the sound of their voices.
I cannot recall one elevated moment in church
Though as a choirboy I pulled in a useful
Sixpence per month.

Strange, that a sense of religion should
Somehow survive all this grim buffoonery!
Perhaps that brisk old person does exist,
And we are living through his Sunday.

D.J. Enright

A REVELATION

A REVELATION

'Set your troubled hearts at rest. Trust in God always; trust also in me. There are many dwelling places in my Father's house; if it were not so I should have told you; for I am going to prepare a place for you. And if I go and prepare a place for you, I shall come again and take you to myself, so that where I am you may be also, and you know the way I am taking.' Thomas said, 'Lord we do not know where you are going, so how can we know the way?' Jesus replied, 'I am the way, the truth, and the life; no one comes to the Father except by me.'

John 14.1-6

First and foremost, I handed on to you the tradition I had received: that Christ died for our sins, in accordance with the scriptures; that he was buried; that he was raised to life on the third day, in accordance with the scriptures; and that he appeared to Cephas, and afterwards to the Twelve. Then he appeared to over five hundred of our brothers at once, most of whom are still alive, though some have died. Then he appeared to James, and afterwards to all the apostles. Last of all he appeared to me too.

1 Corinthians 15.3-8

If the dead are not raised, it follows that Christ was not raised; and if Christ was not raised, your faith has nothing to it and you are still in your old state of sin. It follows also that those who have died within Christ's fellowship are utterly lost. If it is for this life only that Christ has given us hope, we of all people are most to be pitied. But the truth is, Christ was raised to life – the first fruits of the harvest of the dead.

1 Corinthians 15.16-20

I heard a loud voice proclaiming from the throne: 'Now God has his dwelling with mankind! He will dwell among them and they shall he his people, and God himself will be with them. He will wipe every tear from their eyes. There shall be an end to death, and to mourning and crying and pain, for the old order has passed away!'

Revelation 21.3-4

213 For M...

Since I was fourteen
Christ mattered to me.
I cannot say he intervened
but when the dancing horses of my life
spun out of control
I looked for him
standing by the engine with oily fingers.

Now I am no longer young
– and perhaps a little worn –
he hugs me
and dances
and there is lightness in his arms
and there is lightness in his way.
And when I look for him
(as now I often do)...
is it sacrilege to say
Christ has a look of you?

Margaret Cook

214 Disclosure

Prayer is like watching for the
Kingfisher. All you can do is
Be where he is likely to appear, and
Wait.
Often, nothing much happens:
There is space, silence and
Expectancy.
No visible sign, only the
Knowledge that he's been there
And may come again.
Seeing or not seeing cease to matter.
You have been prepared.
But when you've almost stopped
Expecting it, a flash of brightness
Gives encouragement.

Ann Lewin

215 He never expected much

A revelation on my eighty-sixth birthday

Well, World, you have kept faith with me,
    Kept faith with me;
Upon the whole you proved to be
    Much as you said you were.
Since I was a child I used to lie
Upon the leaze and watch the sky,
Never, I own, expected I
    That life would all be fair.

'Twas then you said, and since have said,
    Times since have said,
In that mysterious voice you shed
    From clouds and hills around:
'Many have loved me desperately,
Many with smooth serenity,
While some have shown contempt of me
    Till they dropped underground.

'I do not promise overmuch,
    Child; overmuch;
Just neutral-tinted haps and such,'
    You said to minds like mine.
Wise warning for your credit's sake!
Which I for one failed not to take,
And hence could stem such strain and ache
    As each year might assign.

Thomas Hardy

216 False life

I am no longer afraid of death,
I know well
its dark and cold corridors
leading to life.

I am afraid rather of that life
which does not come out of death
which cramps our hands
and retards our march.

I am afraid of my fear
and even more of the fear of others,
who do not know where they are going,
who continue clinging
to what they consider to be life
which we know to be death!

I live each day to kill death;
I die each day to beget life,
and in this dying unto death,
I die a thousand times and
am reborn another thousand
through that love
from my People,
which nourishes hope.

Julia Esquival, from *Threatened with Resurrection*

217 Back to the cross

Joy ist verboten
in our middle earth of woe
Even to God Himself.

Why should He rejoice
Who made the world so ill
That we must die for it?

Pull down the pillars of the firmament
And bury God within His temple-tomb.
Slam all the gates of Paradise
And seal them with a stone.

Let the searing desert wind
The alien sea
The polar ice in glacial advance
As slow and irresistable as age
Erase
And utterly destroy
This green and living earth
With everything we cherish
All that we love
All we have struggled to achieve
Let it be blotted out as if it had not been.

Is there not cause enough for woe?
And why should He escape?
Drive home the nails
Raise high the cross
Then wait in awe
Trembling
To see what we have done.
Longing
That it could all be otherwise.
Hoping –
How shall we dare to hope?
Hope is the thing that cannot be endured
The thing that breaks us up in tears
Even to think of.

Here is the greatest drama of them all,
The drama of the world upon its cross.
Our world, and us.
We hang there, broken, unconsumed,
Wondering if there is an end.

Such pains we take
Not to be pierced by deadly joy
Whose other name is
God.

W.S. Beattie

218 Death

Who knows the secrets of death?
An exit or an entrance?
The flesh disappears:
The memory lingers on,
Until that too
Falls into oblivion's bottomless pit.

Death:
The front door of heavenly paradise?
The golden gates of eternal utopia?
Or is it a final
Existence-ceasing
End?

John Perry, 13 years

219 Time

Who made time?
Was it God?
Yes! He made all things.
When did he make time?
Yes. When?

He created time at the beginning.
At the beginning of what?
At the beginning of time.
When was that?
Yes. When?

That was before time began.
What was there before?
Nothing, absolutely nothing.
Since when was there nothing?
Yes. Since when?

It was there all the time.

R.F. Enever

220 The junk man

I am glad God saw Death
And gave Death a job taking care of all who are tired of living:
When all the wheels in a clock are worn and slow and the
    connections loose,
And the clock goes on ticking and telling the wrong time
    from hour to hour
And people around the house joke about what a bum clock it is.
How glad the clock is when the big Junk Man drives his wagon
Up to the house and puts his arms round the clock and says:
    'You don't belong here,
    You gotta come
    Along with me,'
How glad the clock is then, when it feels the arms of the
    Junk Man close around it and carry it away.

Carl Sandburg

221 The friend

Since death (properly understood) is the true, ultimate purpose of life, I have for several years past made myself acquainted with this truest and best friend of mankind so that he has for me, not only nothing terrifying any more, but much that is tranquilising and consoling. And I thank God that he has bestowed on me the good fortune of providing the opportunity (you understand me) of recognising death as the key to our true blessedness. I never lie down in my bed without reflecting that perhaps I (young as I am) shall never see another day; yet none of all who know me can say that I am socially melancholy or morose. For this blessing I daily thank my Creator and wish it from my heart for all my fellow man.

W.A. Mozart *in a letter to his dying father*

222 Sing!

If I should go before the rest of you
Break not a flower nor inscribe a stone,
Nor when I'm gone speak in a Sunday voice
But be the usual selves that I have known.

Weep if you must,
Parting is hell,
But life goes on,
So sing as well.

Joyce Grenfell

223 Living death

If you leave me I shall not die,
Nor make grief a trumpet to shatter the sky.
I shall not ask for anything more
Than to walk according to natural law,
One foot behind, the other before.
I shall wake at morning
And sleep at night,
And tell, unfailing,
Black from white.
I shall use my brains
To earn my bread,
Snarl when hungry,
Smile when fed.
I shall not die;
I shall be dead.

Anon

224 After the last breath

There's no more to be done, or feared, or hoped;
None now need watch, speak low, and list, and tire;
No irksome crease outsmoothed, no pillow sloped
    Does she require.

Blankly we gaze. We are free to go or stay;
Our morrow's anxious plans have missed their aim;
Whether we leave to-night or wait till day
    Counts as the same.

The lettered vessels of medicaments
Seem asking wherefore we have set them here;
Each palliative its silly face presents
    As useless gear.

And yet we feel that something savours well;
We note a numb relief withheld before;
Our well-beloved is prisoner in the cell
    Of Time no more.

We see by littles now the deft achievement
Whereby she has escaped the Wrongers all,
In view of which our momentary bereavement
    Outshapes but small.

Thomas Hardy

225 Even rain

Today the lucid mumble and the brave
Send messages to pave their way.
Smiles of the outgoing dangle precariously
Whilst the shy glance up to glance away.
Neighbours stand a foot further from the fence.
But not from reverence.
Faces are replaced by flowers.
Tomorrow, when you are more composed,
They will come in ones and twos.
Even rain, embarrassed from the sky,
Drops soft sporadic showers.

Heather Massie

226 Easter morning Communion

Grief we know about.
But that the heart should be transfixed
By joy,
We hardly dare even to hope.

Just the gardener,
A traveller on the Emmaus road,
A figure on the shore at Galilee.
We see what we expect.

That recognition,
Soul trembling
World remade.

For one imagined moment
My heart is there
As Mary's arms reach out.
She is the word
My silence cannot speak,
And I, bankrupt of love,
Her debtor.

Right now I do not want to think
About some grand scheme of salvation,
Or seek to judge the ways of God.
It is enough.
Why must you burden me, or Him,
With all your dubious theology.
And most of all
Why turn away from Easter Day
To hurry back to Calvary.

The Master has been gone for a whole day.
For a whole lifetime.
Drop everything to welcome him.
Ask this present only.

But no.
"Twas on that night . . . "

I gave My joy to you.
What have you done with it?

Alas
Are we so desperate
Wedded to fear and grief?
Confess it:
Even on Easter Day I shrink from joy.
But I am wrong,
Praise God.

W.S. Beattie

227 Full circle

Your joy had gone;
Your love had spent his time.
Untimely Death had played his part,
His lines were said;
The book of life was
Finished,
Ended.
Good times, bad times,
Rich and poor;
But Death had parted you,
The door between was shut.
Brave thoughts, brave words.
You vowed never to love again;
You said that
Faith and mourning was your part;
And yet inside,
Doubt,
Fear tore your mind,
Despair of life and
Suicide was in your brain.

That night memories filled your head,
They drowned your thought;
Tears wet your cheeks;
The sweetness of recollection
Was bitter in your mouth;
His gentle face,
A knife ripped your soul.
And when the struggle with the
Past was at its end,
Sleep came upon you,
Peace that resolved your fate.

When you woke,
The newly risen sun
Kissed your frosted window.
Strength had returned.
You had the will to live your life,
The courage to be free.
The wheel of time had turned full circle;
And from the ashes of his Death
Was born new Life.

Roger Dunn, 17 years

228 A memory of a sister

The fire advances along the log
 Of the tree we felled,
Which bloomed and bore striped apples by the peck
 Till its last hour of bearing knelled.

The fork that first my hand would reach
 And then my foot
In climbings upward inch by inch, lies now
 Sawn, sapless, darkening with soot.

Where the bark chars is where, one year,
 It was pruned, and bled –
Then overgrew the wound. But now, at last,
 Its growings all have stagnated.

My fellow-climber rises dim
 From her chilly grave –
Just as she was, her foot near mine on the bending limb,
 Laughing, her young brown hand awave.

Thomas Hardy

229 The end?

By sudden accident: a motorway or 'plane,
by darkened shadows from a nuclear bomb,
by anger's warring gunburst;
this way or that,
the end must come.

By poverty and lack of bread,
by persecution of an alien power,
by slow drawn-out and laboured breath,
   natural and timely,
   but heart-stopping;
this way or that,
the end must come.

The end?
Or new beginning?
Do clouds roll back and trumpets sound?
Does Love step out to welcome love,
   revealing all life's meaning
   in one clear burst of light?
Does death end Death
and offer life renewed?

Maybe,
Or maybe not.

We trace the path along a line
   start to end,
   birth to grave,
   one stretched out road.
Perhaps the end is the beginning,
and the beginning, end:
one circle, full complete, and round,
and God within,
without.

Donald Hilton

230 The trumpets sounded

After this it was noised abroad that Mr Valiant-for-truth was taken with a summons by the same post as the other, and had this for a token that the summons was true, That his pitcher was broken at the fountain. When he understood it he called for his friends, and told them of it. Then said he, I am going to my Father's; and though with great difficulty I am got hither, yet now I do not repent me of all the trouble I have been at to arrive where I am. My sword I give to him that shall succeed me in my pilgrimage, and my courage and skill to him that can get it. My marks and scars I carry with me, to be a witness for me that I have fought His battles who now will be my rewarder. When the day that he must go hence was come, many accompanied him to the river side, into which as he went he said, Death, where is thy sting? And as he went down deeper, he said, Grave, where is thy victory? So he passed over, and all the trumpets sounded for him on the other side.

John Bunyan, from *Pilgrim's Progress*

231 Beulah

After this I beheld until they were come into the land of Beulah, where the sun shineth night and day. Here, because they were weary, they betook themselves a while to rest. And because this country was common for pilgrims, and because the orchards and vineyards that were here belonged to the King of the Celestial Country, therefore they were licensed to make bold with any of His things. But a little while soon refreshed them here; for the bells did so ring, and the trumpets continually sound so melodiously, that they could not sleep, and yet they received as much refreshing as if they had slept their sleep never so soundly. Here also all the noise of them that walked the streets was, More pilgrims are come to town! And another would answer, saying, And so many went over the water, and were let in at the golden gates to-day! They would cry again, There is now a legion of shining ones just come to town, by which we know that there are more pilgrims upon the road; for here they come to wait for them, and to comfort them after all their sorrow! Then the pilgrims got up, and walked to and fro; but how were their ears now filled with heavenly noises, and their eyes delighted with celestial visions! In this land they heard nothing, saw nothing, felt nothing, smelt nothing, tasted nothing that was offensive to their stomach or mind; only when they tasted of the water of the river over which they were to go, they thought that it tasted a little bitterish to the palate; but it proved sweeter when 'twas down.

John Bunyan, from *Pilgrim's Progress*

232 In the vineyard?

Go to the market-place, they said,
The owner's taking labour on.
Somehow I missed him, and the day wore by,
An ordinary day, with not much happening.
The sun was hot, I must have gone to sleep.
I had this dream, if dream it was,
That he had come and I was in the vineyard.
People were hard at work, each at his task.
I couldn't find the foreman anywhere.
Not knowing what to do
Because the job was strange to me
I wandered round, trying to look busy.
I saw some weeds, and pulled them up –
At least, I think that they were weeds,
I dug a hole and buried them, in case.
I patched a bit of fencing that looked broken –
Not very well, I hadn't got the tools.
Of course, it maybe wasn't wanted any more.
I fetched and carried for the proper workers
Until I found that I was in their way.
I picked a few stones off the path
That someone might have fallen over.
Various odd things that caught my eye,
But nothing much,
And in the end I got so stuck
I found a quiet corner
And dropped off to sleep again.

When I wake up
Where will I be?
In vineyard or in market-place?
At the day's end
When all the labourers stretch out their hands
Will I have earned a wage?
Or will he say
I had a job for you
But you didn't do it,
You never even found out what it was.
How can I pay you?

W.S. Beattie

233 He comes!

Advent
When God comes
comes again:
maybe an Indian this time
or a Bantu (what do I know?)

When God comes
comes again:
maybe a woman this time
or even a woman-and-man
a couple.

When God comes
comes again:
maybe in the many
the new society
where justice dwells.

When God comes
comes again:
maybe the city of God
the land of the goddess of
reconciliation between
people and nature.

When God comes
comes again:
from one end of the earth
to the other.

Kurt Marti

ACKNOWLEDGEMENTS

The compiler and publishers express thanks for permission to use copyright items. Every effort has been made to trace copyright owners but if any rights have been inadvertently overlooked, the necessary correction will be gladly made in subsequent editions.

Copyright permissions are listed in item order. Where more than one item derives from the same copyright source, item numbers for later entries are indicated in brackets after the first entry.

Item
2 From *The Name* by Karl Rahner. Reprinted by permission of Burns & Oates Ltd/Search Press Ltd
3 From *Moon Tiger* by Penelope Lively. Reprinted by permission of Penguin Books Ltd (first published by Andre Deutsch Ltd), copyright Penelope Lively, 1987
4 Reprinted by permission of the author
6 Reprinted by permission of the author
7 From *The True Wilderness* by H.A. Williams. Reprinted by permission of Harper Collins
10 (17, 18) From *Child Education*. Reprinted by permission of Evans Brothers Ltd
11 Reprinted by permission of Mrs Doe Howard
12 (38, 40, 46, 65, 90, 93) From *Aotearoa Psalms* by Joy Cowley. Reprinted by permission of Catholic Supplies (NZ) Ltd, Wellington, NZ
14 From *Clifton College Writing*, Spring 1969. Reprinted by permission
15 (135) From *At the Rainbow's Foot*. Reprinted by permission of Cambridgeshire Education Department
19 (60, 111, 119, 167, 168) From *Finding the Words*. Reprinted by permission of QA Education Consultancy Services, Cumbria County Council
21 (22, 59) From *Poems from Primary Schools*. Reprinted by permission of the National Association for Teaching English
24 From *Collected Poems* by W.H. Davies. Reprinted by permission of Jonathan Cape and the estate of the author
27 From *Chimney Smoke* by Christopher Morley. Reprinted by permission of Methuen, London
29 (49, 106, 114, 138, 145, 162, 163, 179, 193, 207, 217, 226, 232) Reprinted by permission of the author
31 Reprinted by permission of the World Council of Churches
37 (154, 210) Reprinted by permission of the author
42 From *Words for Worship*, compiled by Campling & Davies. Reprinted by permission of Edward Arnold/Hodder & Stoughton Educational Ltd
44 (78) Reprinted by permission of Christian Education Movement
47 From *Twilight* by Elie Wiesel. Reprinted by permission of Penguin Books Ltd and Editions Grasset & Fasquelle
48 by John L. Bell and Graham Maule; words and music copyright 1989 Iona Community/Wild Goose Publications, Glasgow, Scotland; used by permission
50 (203) Reprinted by permission of the author; 50 appeared in *Reform*
51 From *With One Voice*. Reprinted by permission of Religious Education Press/Chansitor Publications Ltd
53 From *Learning for Life*, Inner London Education Authority
55 (56) From pp 16, 24, 28 of *The Child in the Church*, published by BCC in 1984. Reprinted by permission of the Council of Churches for Britain and Ireland
58 Reprinted by permission of the Head Teacher, Priory Primary School, North Tyneside
61 From *Modern Psalms by Boys* compiled by Raymond Hearn: copyright remains with the author
62 Reprinted by permission of the Acting Headteacher, Breckenbrough School
64 (180, 184, 201) Reprinted by permission of author; 180 from *Tears on the Inside*, published by the author
66 From *The Sun, Dancing* compiled by Charles Causley. Reprinted by permission of Kestrel/Penguin Books Ltd
67 (178, 181, 187, 213, 214, 255) From *New Christian Poetry* edited by Alwyn Marriage. Reprinted by permission of Harper Collins Ltd
68 From *Why, O Lord? Psalms and Poems from Namibia* by Zephania Kameeta, 1986. From Psalm 26 "When the day comes." Reprinted by permission of World Council of Churches, Geneva, Switzerland
69 (98) From *Morning, Noon and Night*. Reprinted by permission of Church Missionary Society (CMS)

74   From *Confessing our Faith Around the World IV. South America 1985: Confession of Faith from a Service for Human Rights, Chile, November 1978.* Reprinted by permission of World Council of Churches, Geneva, Switzerland

75   From *Now*. Reprinted by permission of the author

77   From *One Day in the Life of Ivan Denisovitch* by Alexander Solzhenitsyn, translated into English by Ralph Parker. Reprinted by permission of Victor Gollancz Ltd

80   (81, 82, 83) From *My Shalom, My Peace.* Reprinted by permission of Sabra Books, Tel Aviv

84   (104, 166) Reprinted by permission of Christian Aid. 84 from *Christian Aid News*

85   Reprinted by permission of the author and *Reform*

86   Reprinted by permission of Amnesty International

88   (89) Reprinted by permission of the author

92   From *Interrobang.* by Norman C. Habel. Reprinted by permission of the Lutterworth Press

94   From *Teachers' World.* Reprinted by permission of Evans Brothers Ltd

96   (160, 209) From *The Morning Cockerel Book of Readings,* published by Hart-Davis Educational. Reprinted by permission of Harper Collins

97   From *Arthurian Poems* by Charles Williams. Reprinted by permission of Boydell & Brewer and David Higham Associates

99   From *Sadhana* by Rabindranath Tagore. Reprinted by permission of Macmillan London Ltd

100   From *Francis Kilvert's Diary.* Reprinted by permission of the estate of the author and Chatto & Windus

103   (117, 142, 143) Reprinted by permission of 3M Young Poet Award, 3M UK Ltd

105   From *Heart of Prayer* edited by A. Gittins. Reprinted by permission of Harper Collins

110   From *St Joan* by George Bernard Shaw. Reprinted by permission of the Society of Authors on behalf of the Bernard Shaw estate

113   From the *Wee Worship Book;* copyright 1989 Wild Goose Worship Group/Iona Community, Glasgow, Scotland; used by permission

115   (122) From *The Teilhard Review.* Reprinted by permission of the Teilhard Centre

116   (121) From *The Flowering Tree* by Caryll Houselander. Reprinted by permission of Sheed & Ward Ltd

118   From *Collected Poems* by Edna St Vincent Millay. Reprinted by permission of Harper Collins Ltd

126   From *Up to Date* by Steve Turner. Reprinted by permission of Hodder & Stoughton Ltd

127   From *Ring of Truth* by J.B. Phillips, published by Hodder & Stoughton Ltd

129   From *Christian Life Style* by Edward Patey. Reprinted by permission of EP Publishing and A. & C. Black (Publishers) Ltd

131   From *The Founder of Christianity* by C.H. Dodd. Reprinted by permission of Harper Collins

134   From *Prayers, Poems and Songs* by Huub Oosterhuis. Reprinted by permission of Sheed & Ward Ltd

141   (170, 171, 179) from *Colours of Hope.* Reprinted by permission of Kelling County Primary School, Holt

144   (149) From *Christ in the Concrete City.* Reprinted by the author's permission

148   (227) Reprinted by permission of the Headmaster, Eaton (City of Norwich) School

151   From *True Resurrection* by H.A. Williams. Reprinted by permission of Mitchell Beazley Publishers

157   From *Bread of Tomorrow.* Reprinted by permission of Christian Aid and Revd Jan Berry

161   Reprinted by permission of David Higham Associates

165   (219) From *Poets in School,* published by Harrap; reprinted by permission of the Poetry Society

169   Reprinted by permission of the Headmaster, Hethersett Middle School, Norfolk

173   (183, 196, 202) Reprinted by permission of the author (173 from *Turn but a Stone,* NCEC; 196 from *URC Prayer Handbook*)

174   From *I Weep Before God* by John Wain. Reprinted by permission of Curtis Brown, on behalf of John Wain and Macmillan

175   (176) Reprinted by permission of the Headmistress, Norwich High School (GPDST)

185   From *Earthrights.* Published by the World Wildlife Fund

189   From *Something to Say.* Reprinted by permission of Diocese of Sheffield Board of Education

190   (191) From *Feminine in the Church* edited by Monica Furlong. Reprinted by permission of SPCK (Society for the Promotion of Christian Knowledge)

192   From *Lifelines.* Reprinted by permission of Christian Aid

197   From *Walking on Thorns: The Call to Obedience* by Alan Boesak. Reprinted by permission of World Council of Churches, Geneva, Switzerland

199   From *The Quest for the Historical Jesus* by Albert Schweitzer. Reprinted by permission of A. & C. Black (Publishers) Ltd

204   From *Cider with Rosie* by Laurie Lee. Reprinted by permission of Hogarth Press

205   From *Our Knowledge of God* by John Baillie, OUP 1939. Reprinted by permission of Oxford University Press

206 (208) Reprinted with the permission of the Advisor for Public Affairs to the Archbishop; 206 from a sermon 'The Majesty of God' preached at the Lambeth Conference, 1930

212 From *The Terrible Shears* by D.J. Enright. Reprinted by permission of Watson, Little Ltd

216 From *Threatened with Resurrection*, The Brethren Press, Elgin, Illinois, USA

220 From *Chicago Poems* by Carl Sandburg. Reprinted by permission of Henry Holt & Co. New York

221 From *The Many Faces of Grief* by Edgar N. Jackson, published by SCM Press Ltd

222 Reprinted by permission of Richard Scott Simon Ltd

Bible passages are quoted from *Revised English Bible* © 1989 by permission of Oxford and Cambridge University Presses

INDEX OF AUTHORS

Where the author is not know, the source is given

INDEX OF THEMES

INDEX OF FIRST LINES